Zoey,

MW01688012

Cookie Christmas

Merry Christmas!

Heather Karn

Heather Karn

Cookie Christmas

Scribbling Pen Publishing

Published by Scribbling Pen Publishing
www.scribblingpenpublishing.com

Cover by SLM Creations
www.slmcreations-premadebookcovers.com

To Tobi, without you, this book would not have come about. You gave it life long before I typed the first words.

Chapter 1

Sleigh bells rang. Lights glimmered. Snowflakes drifted from the sky. The scent of gingerbread wafted through the air. Carols echoed through the streets while children ran by with sticky faces from the candy canes they held in their hands. It was the perfect Christmas scene…at the beginning of October.

Humans could think what they wanted to about Christmas all year round, but for a Christmas elf, the scene was completely normal. Even the dragons flying high above Christmas Village pulling Santa's sleigh was a normal sight. They were Ice Dragon Shifters, and they provided Santa and the elves with protection, and a way for Santa to deliver his presents all in one night.

"Are you coming, Holly? Or should I tell Papa that you'll be late because you're daydreaming again?" my twin sister, Jolly, quipped while grabbing my arm and hauling me after her up the red brick street. The last few days had seen warmer weather, which had melted the snow so the brick was visible. That only happened once a year, if at all.

I shook her hand from my arm. "I wasn't daydreaming. I was thinking."

"About what? And don't you dare lie to me. I know when you're lying."

"Really? Like how you knew I was lying about Sparkle being the one to wrap you and your bed in garland while you slept when it was actually me?" For being Christmas elves, my sister and I spent most of the year on Santa's Naughty List. Somehow we always managed to make the Good List just before Christmas every year. It was quite impressive. Our parent's didn't think so.

"Okay, I missed that one, but you can't blame me. I was rather preoccupied with something more important." Jolly flipped her red-streaked brown hair over her shoulder, which was her way of ending the conversation. She did not want me to bring up her recent flirtations with one of the elves who worked at the Wrapping Warehouse.

Shoving my hands into the pockets of my wool coat, I shivered against the chill breeze that raced down the street. The heat wave that had melted the snow had passed, and in its wake was a cold snap that chilled me to the bone. The cold was the only part of living here that I disliked, but if it meant I could be surrounded by Christmas all year long, I wouldn't complain about it- at least not out loud.

"What did Papa want to talk to you about anyway?" Jolly asked as we neared the Bakery.

Mama and Papa had sat us down at the beginning of the year and told us we would officially need to choose a location to work instead of bouncing around to whatever job we felt like that day. We'd both chosen to work at the bakery, but I was sure Jolly only chose that job because I had chosen first and she didn't want to leave me. I couldn't blame her. As much as I loved baking and helping Papa, I would have followed her had she given her preference first.

I shrugged. "I have no idea what he wants. He just said that I needed to come to his office at noon after he returns from his morning meeting with Santa. It probably has something to do with candy cane bits I snuck into the chocolate chip cookies last week."

"I heard those were pretty tasty," Jolly giggled, pulling the door to the bakery open. The bell above the door rang, but not an elf inside looked up. They were all too busy preparing for the day's baking tasks.

I walked inside when Jolly held the door for me. "They were, but I'm sure Papa wasn't happy about it. You know how he loves order and everything to go as planned. One cookie sheet out of place makes him crazy."

"True. Well, good luck. The schedule says I'm on sugar cookie detail...again." She shook her head, eyeing the schedule hanging on the wall. Her less than enthusiastic tone told me she'd much rather be working for Horace delivering Christmas trees than baking the sugar cookies. That was a job I certainly wouldn't want.

"Why don't you just switch to a different building? I'm sure you'll be happier than working here."

Her lips buzzed as she pushed air out between them in an

awkward sigh, or something. It was Jolly. Who knew what her sounds meant. "I don't want to leave you, Holly. It's no fun getting into trouble by myself. Plus, there's no one to blame it on if it's only me."

There was truth to that. "Well then, head upstairs. I've got inventory duty again."

My sister shuddered. "That could quite possibly be worse than baking sugar cookies."

"I don't mind. At least I do it right. Razzle can't do an accurate count to save his life. That butter shortage last month was all his fault. I thought Papa was going to throw him in an oven."

"Talking about Razzle, huh?" Peppercorn piped up, looking over my shoulder at her schedule. Like us, she always arrived just on time for her shift to start. I liked showing up early, but I usually had to drag Jolly out the door.

I nodded, unbuttoning my coat. "Yup. Speaking of Razzle, I haven't seen him in a while. Well, since the butter incident."

Peppercorn leaned in close, glanced around to make sure no one else was within earshot, and whispered, "I heard he was transferred to toy repair."

Jolly and I gasped, and I placed a hand over my skipping heart. Few elves were ever sent to toy repair. No one had ever volunteered for the position. If you were one of the unlucky few who made it to that department, it meant you'd messed up above and beyond the call of duty. A shortage of Christmas cookies because of no butter must have qualified as a huge mistake...unless there was more to the story that we weren't privy to.

Any other day, I would have suggested that we snoop around to find out what we could about Razzle's demotion. Instead, I was already behind schedule to start doing inventory since I needed to take time out of my day to meet with Papa. Right now, work came first. Play would have to wait.

That thought froze my fingers as they moved to release the last button on my coat. Standing straight, I found my brain wouldn't move past the new realization of what I'd thought. Jolly arched a brow at me, but that was all I could comprehend in my current state.

"You okay?" she asked, eyeing me like I was a crazy person. Taking my shoulders, she steered me away from the schedule board, which was becoming crowded as the last minute bakery elves walked through the door and headed toward it. "You look like you've seen a ghost or something. Do you need to sit down?"

My head shook, but I wasn't in control of it. I should have sat down, but I reassured Jolly that I was fine and truddged toward the back of the building where our supplies were stored. After dropping my coat off in the supplies office, I grabbed my clipboard and strode into the store room, which was basically a large warehouse attached to the bakery, only it was nicer than any warehouse I'd ever heard about.

Industrial refrigerators and freezers lined the walls, all stocked full of baking supplies. Row after row of shelving held other baking ingredients from flour and sugar, to chocolate chips and dried fruit. It wasn't only cookies the bakery supplied Christmas Village and the stores around Earth with. Anything that could be baked was represented, especially breads, cakes, and pies.

The smells coming from inside the bakery drifted to me, making my stomach rumble. I'd missed breakfast this morning because Papa had mentioned needing to talk to me before I could eat. After that, nerves took over. I wouldn't tell Jolly just how nervous I was that Papa wanted to talk to me at work instead of talking to me at his home office.

Add to those nerves that a few minutes ago I'd actually had an adult thought. A mature thought. I'd decided that I wanted to put work before any childish schemes. That wasn't me. That wasn't normal. The real me would never have had that thought. It was scandalous, and there was no way I could mention it to Jolly.

"You skipped breakfast," I muttered to myself as I began to count cases of canned pumpkin. "It's your brain being sugar deprived. Yeah, that's it. All you need is a few cookies to get your brain juices flowing in the right direction."

Before starting on the cases of powdered sugar, I slipped inside and stole a few strawberry chocolate chip muffins. With any luck, those would give my brain the energy it needed to come up with an idea to add me back on the Naughty List for the next month.

By the time noon rolled around, I hadn't come up with a single bad idea that sounded appealing in any way. However, I was on schedule to finish the inventory by quitting time, even with my meeting with Papa taking time out of my day.

When I reached his office on the top floor of the bakery, I found he hadn't yet returned from his meeting with Santa. So, I sat in one of three chairs sitting outside his office door and waited for him. While I tried to keep my focus on finding some practical joke to play on my friends, my mind kept wandering back to my inventory. We were low on eggs, and more chocolate chips had been used than usual. A little snitch had probably made off with a few bags. As long as we didn't run low, Papa wouldn't care. We were sugar addicts after all.

My foot had begun tapping with anticipation by the time Papa jogged up the stairs to his office's landing. He carried a large, black binder in his hand that was almost too big for him. When he caught sight of me, he glanced at his watch.

"Wow, I am late, aren't I? Well, there's a first for everything, I suppose," he told me, breathless from his jog up the stairs. Papa was rarely late for anything, but I wouldn't question him since he'd been meeting with Santa.

"How did your meeting go?" I asked as he opened his office door and I followed him inside.

Book cases lined both sides of the room, filled mostly with dessert cookbooks and Christmas stories. His desk sat on the other side of the room with two plush chairs sitting in front of it. A computer monitor sat on one side of the desk, leaving most of the space open, and that open space was covered in papers. A large bay window took up most of the wall behind the desk, letting in what little sunlight we could soak in at the North Pole.

Papa crossed the room after he let me inside and set his binder on the desk. I didn't come to his office much, so I sought out his new books. One was filled with delicious looking pastries. Another was of every way you could think of to cook chicken. I swallowed a laugh. Papa loved all cookbooks, not just baked goods.

"Take a seat, Holly." He waved to one of the two open chairs on the other side of his desk. Obviously, he was in business mode. The last time I'd been in his office and he'd acted this way, he'd questioned me about the butter shortage. This did not bode well for me.

I sat on the front of the chair's seat, ready to bolt if necessary. "Umm, am I in trouble?"

Papa chuckled as he sorted through some paperwork on his desk and pulled more from the binder he'd brought with him from his meeting. "No, darling, you aren't in trouble. Since what I wish to discuss with you is business related, and is far more important than schedule changes, I thought it would be best if we discussed it here instead of at home."

Butterflies swarmed in my stomach like they had this morning. My gut had been right when I'd thought it had to be important if he'd wanted to talk to me here instead of at home. Even though he'd reassured me that I wasn't in trouble, I had a difficult time believing it. Unless he was giving me a promotion? I pushed that thought away. Promotions were for mature adults, and I hadn't done anything to deserve a promotion.

He found the piece of paper he'd been searching for and placed it on the desk in front of himself before clasping his hands and leaning forward. "As you know, the bakery has been having trouble keeping up with supply and demand. We're barely making enough cookies and other baked goods to fill the orders coming in from the human companies we sell to. After all these years, they still don't know they're purchasing cookies from the North Pole. Anyway, there were more than usual orders last year, and we predict there will be even more this year."

I nodded. It was all Papa had been thinking about, and talking about, for the last few months. Mama had gone as far as forbidding the topic at the dinner table after the first month he'd stewed about it over our nightly meal. But what did this have to do with me?

"Santa and I have come up with a solution that we believe will work to solve this problem. However, it will take a lot of hard work, dedication, and time."

I nodded again, becoming impatient. "But what does this have to do with me?"

"Patience, Holly, I'm getting to that." Papa stood and walked around his desk to sit in the vacant chair beside me. "The plan is to open a second bakery. This one will be in New York City. It will have easy access to a vast majority of Earth since it is one of the large hubs of transportation. However, we want to have it open and running at full steam by November first, right on time for the holiday rush."

Well, that was a good idea. A second bakery would help ease the pressure off this one.

I leaned back in my chair. "So you want me to help out here while you start the other bakery? Is that why you wanted to meet with me?"

Papa's smile was almost pained when he shook his head. "No. Not quite. I won't be leaving this bakery. What I discussed with Santa, and he agreed with, was sending you down to New York to run the second bakery. The building is already purchased and equipment is being installed as we speak. You'll leave this week. There isn't time to waste."

Chapter 2

Wait. What? He wanted me to open the new bakery in New York City? Me? The one who just this past April Fools Day filled our bathtub to the brim with cranberry jelly? On top of that, he wanted it opened by November first? That was only three and a half weeks away!

"Holly? You okay?" Papa asked, reaching between us to take my hand. That was the second time today someone had asked me if I was okay. I was beginning to think that maybe I wasn't. This had to be a bad dream. Yeah, that's what it was.

"You're serious?" I squeaked, pinching myself with my free hand to wake myself up. When it didn't work, I assumed I really was awake.

Papa sighed and leaned back in his chair. "Yes, I'm serious. Santa and I both agreed that you are the perfect choice."

"But I don't know how to run a bakery! And I don't know anything about New York."

"You'll learn. We have faith in you, Holly. Of all the elves who work here, you have the most enthusiasm for the job, and you love to bake. You're growing up. Also, I'm not leaving you alone. You'll have an assistant. He's already there supervising the equipment installation"

Shrugging my shoulders, I shook my head at my father. "If he's already there, why doesn't he just lead this bakery then?"

"Because he's never worked in a bakery before in his life. He's studied business and will be able to help you with ordering and other vital tasks, but this is your forte, not his."

"But Papa, it isn't my forte. I don't know the first thing about running a bakery. I just do what I'm told."

He patted my hand, his voice becoming gentle. "I have faith in you. If I didn't know with all my heart that you could do this, I wouldn't be sending you. And don't forget, I'm still here. In fact, I'll be spending your first week with you in New York to help you settle in."

If that was supposed to comfort me, it didn't. One week was all I'd have him for, and then I'd be alone. I wouldn't even have Jolly, would I?

"Jolly?" I knew he'd understand what I asked, and I received my answer when his lips turned down in a frown.

"She's staying here. All of the elves in this bakery are staying. The elves that you'll manage don't live at the North Pole."

This news startled a gasp from me. "You're talking about the elves stationed in Texas? I thought they only did studies of popular toy trends and other paperwork like that."

Papa nodded and stood, pacing his office. "Yes, most of them have clerical and accounting backgrounds, which is why Merric is the perfect assistant for you."

Merric. So that was his name. I crossed my fingers, hoping he was a nice elf. And patient.

"You'll need to train some of your elves to bake," Papa continued, "but they're elves, so they should pick up the skills needed within a short time. You have just over three weeks. You can do this."

"Do I have a choice?"

My question startled Papa, and he turned to me with furrowed brows. "I've never known you to back down from a challenge."

"Papa, do I have a choice?"

He sighed and rubbed the back of his neck. The sun glinted off his black hair, and I realized for the first time how much gray was splattered throughout. Deep wrinkles and dark smudges under his eyes showed his stress: he wasn't sleeping. Not well anyway. He needed help or he was going to burn out.

"Never mind." I stood from my seat and crossed the room to him and took his hands in mine. "I'm sure you know what you're doing. Remember, if this doesn't work, I told you so."

"It will work," he reassured me, squeezing my hands. "Christmas is about miracles, and miracles happen when you least expect them."

"Does Mama know?"

"Yes, I told her last night. She's sad to see you leave, but she's excited for your new opportunity. We decided to let you tell Jolly, so why don't the two of you take the rest of the day off. Spend some time together."

My sigh could have woken the dead. "She isn't going to take this well."

"No, she won't, but maybe now she'll actually transfer to a position she likes. She's been nothing but a grump since she started working here full-time."

I couldn't agree more with that statement. Leaning close, I circled my arms around his waist in a tight hug. "I won't let you down, Papa."

"I know you won't, Holly." He hugged me back tighter. When I stepped away, a fine mist filled his eyes. Clearing his throat, Papa blinked away the moisture. "Now, I'll need you to be here first thing tomorrow morning. There are some details we need to discuss before you leave."

Papa walked me to the door and opened it. My voice shook. "I'll see you tonight. Wish me luck telling Jolly."

"Good luck. You'll need it."

Usually I skipped down the stairs two at a time. Today, I trudged down the two flights to the floor where the sugar cookies were made. It was one of the two floors that never changed flavors. The other was gingerbread cookies.

Jolly was across the room, singing at the top of her lungs with Flick, her usual baking partner. How those two ever baked their required number of cookies in a day, I couldn't begin to guess. They were always horsing around when I caught sight of them on various trips to their work floor.

My twin sister caught sight of me and waved both of her arms for me to join them. I tried, but my feet wouldn't move. No matter how hard I tried, I couldn't cross the room. I couldn't even manage one step in her direction. How do you tell your sister and best friend in the whole of the North Pole that you'll be leaving and didn't have any idea when you'd return, or if you ever would?

Swallowing hard, I pivoted on my heel and walked right back through the door I'd just entered. This time, I raced down the stairs to the main floor. A door thudded shut a few flights above, which alerted me to Jolly's presence. I didn't stop, but flew through the front door of the building, nearly knocking over a pair of dragon shifters who were about to enter.

"Oops, I'm sorry. Excuse me." I didn't look to see who it was I'd almost ran into, but tried to move past them so I could run home and lock myself in my bedroom.

"Holly, what's wrong?" my other best friend, Vixen asked, grabbing my shoulder and stopping me in my tracks. At well over five feet in her human form, she dwarfed my four and a half feet. Her companion was even taller.

"Where's the fire?" Vixen's mate, Lunar, asked, eyeing the building like he was searching for flames.

"Where are you going?" Jolly demanded, her small frame filling the bakery's doorway. "You're acting awfully strange today, Holly. Spill. What's happening?"

"It wasn't my idea. I had nothing to do with it," I blurted before slapping a hand over my mouth. Jolly's eyes widened and the dragon shifters both folded their arms. Vix was already beginning to mimic her mate. With a calm, deep breath, I lowered my hand. "We need to talk, Jolly. It's important, and you aren't going to like it."

"Okay, now you really are scaring me." She stepped outside, letting the door close behind her. Her eyes shown with worry, and even Lunar's eyes narrowed. He'd joined the ice dragon shifter clan last December, and since then he'd only ever seen me happy or annoyed. Even Vix had never seen me like this, whatever this was besides nervous and scared.

The butterflies that had been swimming and twirling in my stomach in Papa's office were back, and they'd invited more friends to join them. Without a word of consolation, I led the way back to our house. Mama was gone. She worked part-time making tinsel and today was a work day, which meant we had the house to ourselves. Even still, I led my sister and friends to our bedroom.

Vixen and Lunar took the couch, cuddling close together while I hopped onto my bed. Sitting against the wall, I hugged a stuffed toy reindeer to me, clinging to it like it was a lifeline. Jolly sat beside me and the room grew silent.

"How's the new house?" I asked the pair seated on the couch.

Instead of building their own place, they'd moved into an already built house after the dragons who'd inhabited it had decided to move and form their own clan further to the east.

"Nope, you go first. What has you so spooked?" Vix leaned away from Lunar, and Jolly shifted to sit closer to me.

My gaze drifted down to the plush toy in my arms. "I've got a new job."

"And?" Jolly prodded, poking me in the arm. "What is it?"

Taking a gasping breath, I blurted out my news. "I'm going to be running Papa's new bakery. It's in New York City. I leave within the week."

Dead silence greeted my announcement, and I was sure they could each hear my pounding heart. "What? I think I misheard you. Can you repeat that?" Jolly twisted fingers in her ears as if to clean them out so she could hear better. "Did you just say you're moving to New York City?"

"Yup. That's what I said."

"You can't go."

"Jolly, I have to."

"No, you don't," she argued, grabbing my face so I was forced to stare at her. "No, you do not have to go. You tell Papa no. You will not leave me, Holly."

Tears streamed down Jolly's face, and her words became slurred as she fought to talk through sobs. Her hands were wet on my face from the tears that slid down my cheeks. An ache grew in my chest making it difficult to breathe. I grabbed my sister, pulling her to me, and together we held one another and sobbed. Already the loneliness of leaving her closed in around me. What was I doing? I couldn't leave her, I just couldn't. But I had to. I had to help Papa, and not just Papa, but Santa as well.

I wiped tears from Jolly's cheeks when we released each other after there were no more tears to be shed. "You will be brave, Jolly. Mama and Papa are going to need you to be brave. To be strong. I need you to be strong." I couldn't do this if she fell apart again, and I had to do this.

Jolly nodded and wiped the dampness from my face. "I'll try. But it's so far away."

"It is, but it could be farther, and I'm sure Papa will let you visit, and I'm sure I can come home too. I just don't know how often." I set my hands on her shoulders. "And now you can choose whatever job you want, because we all know that you're only working at the bakery because of me."

Jolly nodded, a giggle breaking her solemn mood. "Yeah, that's right. I suppose I can choose a different job, but not until after you leave."

"That's fair." A sniffle stopped me, and both Jolly and I glanced over to the couch where Vixen sat curled into Lunar's side, her face buried in his shoulder. He held her, his hand rubbing her back. Jolly wasn't the only person I would be leaving who I cared about and who cared for me. "Vixen, are you okay?"

She nodded, not removing her face from Lunar's shirt. His eyes were red, but his cheeks were dry.

Lunar smiled at me, but it trembled. "We're happy for you, Holly, but we'll miss you as well. Try not to burn the new bakery down, would you?"

I couldn't help it: I stuck my tongue out at him. Lunar chuckled and Vix lifted her head to find out what he laughed at. When she saw my reaction to his teasing, she smacked him in the stomach with an order to behave.

"You said you leave this week?" Vixen asked and cleared her throat.

My shoulders sunk. "Yup. That's what Papa said. He didn't give an exact day, so I suppose once he goes over what he wants to tell me tomorrow and I finish packing, we'll be on our way. He's coming down for a week or two to make sure I settle in. After that, I'll be working with Merric."

Jolly's eyes lit up. "Ooo, who's Merric? You didn't mention you'd be working with someone!"

"Seriously, Jolly, for all we know he's married with five children."

She winked. "Or he's single and perfectly eligible. I like to be positive."

"You like to be a pain in the butt."

"No more than you, and no less either."

I stared around my room. My time sleeping here was coming to an end. What would my new room look like? Would it be somewhere in the city? There was still so much I didn't know, but I would ask Papa in the morning. Swallowing hot tears, I crawled off the bed and strode straight to our movie selection.

"Well, I want to watch a movie. Sorry, Vix, but I'm in the mood for Rudolph."

Vixen groaned behind me. She hated the movie, but it was my favorite, and I wanted to watch it with my best friends one more time before I left. After slipping the movie in the player, I turned on our TV, and Jolly and I squished on the couch with the two dragons. Lunar never minded squishing. It meant he could be closer to Vixen.

We laughed. We cried. We sang every song at the top of our lungs, no matter how off tune it came out. Even Vixen joined us for a song or two. Lunar had seen the movie with us enough to be able to sing nearly every song. For a dragon, he had a remarkable voice.

Mama stuck her head in the room as the movie's ending credits rolled across the screen. She laughed with us when Vixen cheered, throwing her hands into the air as she always did when Rudolph finished. I went to switch movies, and caught sight of Mama in the doorway.

"Hi, Mama."

"Hello, Holly. Papa says he spoke to you today. He's worried about you two girls and wanted me to check on you."

Jolly hopped up on the couch and turned to face our mother. "We wanted to light bomb Vixen's house, but we thought it was a bad idea considering Holly is supposed to behave now." Light bombing was the same concept as humans toilet papering someone's house, and we'd done it too many times to count.

I shook my head at Jolly, mimicking Mama's reaction to her. When Jolly wanted to hide her feelings, she made off the wall, silly comments. The sillier the remark, the stronger the feelings she was hiding.

"Behave, Jolly," Mama warned her. "The last time you did that, you almost didn't make the Good List in time for Christmas."

Jolly grumbled and I laughed. That had been the closest we'd come to being on the Naughty List on Christmas day. Since then, we'd been more careful about our pranks and timing them well before Christmas Eve.

"Does Holly have to go?" my sister asked Mama, who nodded again.

"Yes, she does. It will be a great experience for her. You will both survive this change, I promise. Now, let me update your father, and let's all go to the square. The choir is performing this afternoon, and I want to hear their new songs."

Lunar stood and helped Vixen to her feet. "We wish we could join you, but Merlin wanted to discuss clan business with us before dinner. Now is as good a time as ever to get that over with."

"We'll see you later, Holly. Don't you dare leave without saying goodbye," Vixen warned.

I leapt into my friends arms and squeezed her in a tight bear hug. "I wouldn't dream of it."

Chapter 3

I didn't wait until my shift started to meet Papa in his office. He always arrived well before start time to look over the schedule, sort through his papers, and any other tasks he felt needed to be completed before the other elves showed up for work. Since I'd woken early and hadn't fallen back to sleep, I dressed and accompanied Papa to work. Today I didn't bother checking the schedule. I wouldn't be on it. The idea was strange, and did nothing to calm my nerves.

"Papa, so what exactly am I supposed to do? I'm not good with money, and I have no idea how that works in the human world." I slid into the same chair I'd occupied the day before while he turned his computer on.

Shaking his head, he turned his attention to me. "No, that will be Merric's responsibility. He's had the training and can manage it all. What you are responsible for is the day to day running of the bakery, like making sure all the orders are filled on time and that everyone has a job to do. Elves are not easily managed. Most would rather play than work, and you'll find some like certain jobs over others. However, for now, you'll be interviewing job candidates and making sure that all equipment is installed and ready to go by the deadline. Oh, and to make sure your inventory is fully stocked. If you need anything, fill out the order form and hand it off to Merric. He will order it for you."

I was glad I was sitting. This job was much bigger than I'd anticipated. More and more I was glad that I would have an assistant.

"Is Merric already there, or when does he arrive at the bakery?" I played with a loose string on my shirt sleeve while waiting for Papa's answer.

Papa's fingers tapped on the keyboard. "He's already there. He has been for a few weeks." His fingers paused their tapping. "You'll find he's quite capable, but he's not nearly as full of energy as most elves. He loves Christmas, but he keeps it better contained."

"Oh. What about his family? Does he have a wife and kids?"

The tapping continued again. "Nope. He's single, in his early twenties, and he's never been to Canada, let alone the North Pole."

My face fell into my hands and I groaned. "If Jolly asks, he's in his late sixties, has a wife, three children, and eight grandchildren, okay?"

"That specific, huh?"

"It's best we're both telling her the same lies, so yes, that specific."

"Holly, lying puts you on the Naughty List. The head of this Bakery and the manager for the new bakery can't have their names on the Naughty List." A smile quirked at the corners of his mouth. "However, if asked, I'll defer the answer to you. Will that work?"

"Yup, and I'll tell her to ask you. I'm sure we can keep her busy chasing her tail until after I leave."

"And this is why your mother and I try to stay off you girls' bad side. You can be quite evil in a passive aggressive way. Now, come over here and let me show you the building's blue prints so you know where everything is located."

Standing, I walked around his desk so that I could see the monitor. "While we're at it, can you tell me where I'll be living?"

"Yes, why don't we start with that? Your apartment, office, and a conference room are on the top floor of the bakery's tower. Everyone else will be living in a smaller building next to the bakery, including Merric. I wanted you to be able to have privacy. Is this all right?" Papa glanced over at me. Was it all right?

"For now, yes, I like it. We'll see what happens as we go along."

"Good, now the first five floors are cookies, the next five are…" He continued to explain what each floor was used for, all the way down to the baking supplies that were in three basement levels. By the time Papa was done, my brain was buzzing from information overload.

"That's a lot to take in," I explained, sinking back down into the chair I'd left to view his documents. "Do you have copies of all of this? Paper documents, that is." I didn't have a cell phone, tablet, or computer. I'd never needed one. It appeared I may need to ask for one.

Papa read my mind. "No, but here's a tablet I procured just for you. I've already uploaded all the building schematics and documents. You'll find a program for entering inventory, calculating how many supplies you need for each order, and how long each order should take to complete. Also, there's an app that one of the tech elves made for creating a schedule. We're putting a lot of new technology into this venture, and if it works for you, we may begin to implement it here as well. Merric has an identical tablet with nearly the same information. If you become confused, go to him for help. He's a technological whiz."

I stared at the tablet he handed me. It was black and sleek, and I had no idea what to do with it. At best, I knew how to run a DVD player. Sure, I'd seen plenty of technological toys since I helped wrap them, but I'd never been allowed to actually touch or play with one.

"Everything you need is on that device. Spend some time poking around on it. Oh, and we created an email address for you. Here, let me show you."

Papa spent the next two hours showing me all of the handy tools the tablet offered. When he opened my new email account, a message was already in the inbox from one Merric Huntington. Papa didn't ask me to open the email, and I didn't offer. I preferred that our first correspondence was done in private.

When our tutorial was finished, Papa took me on a tour of the bakery and pointed out everything I would need to know from a manager's point of view. By the time we were finished, my stomach was in knots and my brain was mush. I was way in over my head, but there was no way to back out gracefully now that I'd committed myself to do the job.

"And that wraps up today's lesson," Papa laughed, clapping me on the back when all I could do was stare at the paperwork strewn on a table in the warehouse. It was the order forms he used. He'd been showing me how to calculate how much inventory I should have on hand for each project. While it was in a program on my tablet, he didn't trust technology to do it right, though I wasn't to mention that to Merric.

After I was released to go home and soak in what I'd learned that day, Papa headed back to his office. Instead of going home as directed, I grabbed my coat and found a quiet corner in the warehouse. The first task was to find a place to sit, which ended up being a chest freezer in a far corner. I laid my coat on top of it and hoisted myself up and sat on it, hoping it would provide a bit of comfort. It didn't, but I was already sitting so I pulled up my email account.

My finger hovered over Merric's message, titled, "Interviews." When I finally gained the courage to tap the email, a brief note was enclosed.

"Holly, I look forward to meeting you. Chip has had me schedule interviews for various positions in the bakery. I thought it best if I waited until you arrived so that we could both sit in on them. I'm not much of a baker, so you would know better questions to ask for those positions anyway. Also, we're a week or two behind with equipment installation, but by the time we finish hiring, the equipment should be ready to use. If there is anything you need from me before you arrive, please let me know. Safe travels. – Merric."

I didn't like that we were already behind schedule. That didn't bode well for the project. It took me a moment to remember how to reply to a message, but I did and quickly typed back a note.

"Hi Merric, I'll see you in a few days. Thank you for the updates. Did anyone build any extra time into the deadline in case we fell behind? We can start interviews the day after I arrive, I suppose. Papa will be joining us for the first week, maybe the next as well, but you probably know that already. Well, I need to go pack. Bye. – Holly."

I clicked send without rereading the message, knowing that if I did reread it I would never be able to send it. With my first email on its way to the recipient, I pulled up the web browser and began searching for information on New York City. I had never wanted to go there, I'd never wanted to leave home, so I'd never done any research about the place. It wasn't like I was there to be a tourist, and I wouldn't have time to see the sights, at least not right away. I just wanted to know what to expect from my new hometown.

After a half an hour of research, I closed the browser and was about to shut the screen off on the tablet when a new email message popped up. Of course it was from Merric. I didn't hesitate to open it, ready to read what he had to say.

"I made a schedule of deadlines we must meet in order to open on time, and then I bumped those up, so we do have some flexibility. However, I would prefer to stay ahead of schedule. The top floor of the bakery was completed first, so your space is available and ready to use. Right now I'm working out of your office until you come. Mine is a floor below yours, but it's not quite finished yet. I hope you don't mind. – Merric."

A stupid grin curved across my lips. If Jolly were here she'd start teasing me, and the thought of that made me blush. I'd never met the elf, and for all I knew he couldn't sing, throw a snowball, or wrap a present in under a minute. All of those qualities were a necessity, and were at the top of my husband requirement list. Jolly and I had both made one when we turned eighteen. If he couldn't do those three simple things, then he was cut from the running. After all, those were important characteristics for any elf. Right?

"That's fine, Merric. Use my office for as long as you need. I probably won't know what to do with it yet anyway. Can you send me a list of those deadlines? – Holly"

I waited for a response after sending the email, but when one didn't come, I let the screen go dark. Frowning, and a bit bummed that he hadn't responded back right away, I slid off the freezer and pulled my coat on. In my nervous excitement yesterday, I'd left it here. It had been a frigid walk to work, and I refused to leave my coat again.

Halfway to the exit, the tablet dinged. My feet stopped. That was the sound it had made when Merric's last email came through. Not wanting to wait to read his reply, I turned the screen on and navigated to my email. All the excitement coursing through me drained in an instant, leaving cold disappointment in its wake. Yes, I had an email, but it was from Papa. It was about travel arrangements, which I could read about later.

Then another ding and a new email popped up. My stomach dipped. This one was from Merric.

"Cool, thanks. I appreciate the use of the office. And yeah, I'll send you the file with the deadlines. I'll have to send it tomorrow. Our delivery of cookie sheets just got here and it's going…well, interesting."

Interesting? That couldn't be good. I wasn't looking forward to leaving my friends and family, but I was so ready to take control of this job and know what was happening in New York. "Interesting" wasn't enough detail to keep me from thinking the worst.

"When you have a chance, can you explain what 'Interesting' means? Thanks." I sent the message and finished my walk through the warehouse.

I was already through the door, heading for the exit, when I heard Jolly's voice as she and Flick crashed through the stairwell doorway. It was quitting time, and before I could turn and run, Jolly spotted me. Her voice carried above everyone else's as she called to me.

"Hey, Holly, we were just going to...what is that?" she pointed at the tablet, and I sighed. My sister was about to become green, and it wasn't a good color on her.

"It's a tablet. Papa gave it to me for my new job. And no, you can't see it. It's private."

Jolly grabbed me by the shoulders and shook me. "Are you serious? How can you have one of those and not show it to me?"

Because there were emails from Merric on it, that was why. "Because you'll go crazy and I'll never get it back. Face it, you have a bad track record for pulling that."

She paused, thinking about it for a brief moment. When she grinned back, I wanted to run. "Yes, but you don't have a spotless record either, my companion in trouble. Should I tell Papa who it was that snuck a drone out of its box and flew it around Christmas Village with a banner attached that said 'Humbug'?"

I gasped, my hand flying to my mouth. "You wouldn't. Jolly, that's blackmail. And I'm sure he already knows."

"Let's go find out."

I let her make it as far as the stairwell before I called for her to stop. If Papa didn't know it was me who'd flown the drone, I didn't want him to find out now. Not like this.

"You are evil, Jolly. Pure evil."

She skipped back to me, a giggle tinkling around the room. "No, I'm fun. There's a big difference. Now, hand it over."

"You're too bossy for your own good," I warned, passing the tablet over to her against my better judgment.

She scrolled around different apps, never lingering on any one item. Then she found one that interested her. My heart stuttered.

"Ooo, email." Her finger dove for the email icon.

"Don't!" I snatched away the device before she made contact with the screen.

Jolly stared wide-eyed at my reaction, her finger pointed out into space. It took her several seconds to register what had happened, and she blinked several times before lowering her hand. Then the worst possible reaction occurred: she smiled. It wasn't a normal smile. It was a devilish, you're hiding something and I want to know about it, smile.

"Let me guess: Merric."

Chapter 4

I clung to the tablet, refusing to let her see it again after her observation. "Yes, Merric. And Papa. Now, what were you telling me before you noticed this?"

She shook her head. "No way. You have to tell me all the juicy details, like why your cheeks are glowing bright red. Are you blushing, dear sister of mine?"

"No," I argued. "It's hot in here, is all. Now what were you going to say?"

"Oh, that. Well, it's nothing as exciting as Merric, but we were planning a snowball fight tonight. What do you think? Are you interested?"

I hesitated, thought about it, and shook my head. "Sorry, Jolly, not this time."

Her hands balled on her hips as she glared at me. "So, what? You get a big promotion and suddenly you're no fun anymore?"

"It's not like that, Jolly. I'm stressed out and nervous, and a snowball fight will only make that worse. If you want me to join you, I'd be happy to make some snow angels. We haven't done that in forever."

Jolly crossed her arms while Flick eyed her, waiting to see what she would say. "You know, a snowball fight would be epic right now, but since you're determined to ruin my fun, snow angels it is. First, I want a muffin. Let's go grab one."

TWO DAYS LATER, Jolly and I stood arm in arm, staring down at the snow angels we'd made moments before, both of us trying not to cry. Papa and Mama were loading my belongings into the back of the elve's sleigh. It was tiny compared to Santa's large Christmas sleigh, but it fit elves perfectly, and I didn't have much to bring with me to New York. Since the sleigh was small, it required only one dragon to pull it, and Vixen had volunteered to pull the sleigh. Lunar would fly shotgun, as he called it, since he wouldn't let Vix come alone. After she'd been kidnapped last Christmas, Lunar had barely let her out of his sight.

"Do you have to go? Can't you stay? Why didn't they build another bakery up here?" Jolly blubbered before blowing her nose into one of the fifty tissues she'd stashed in her multitude of coat pockets.

I cupped her chilly, damp face in my hands. "Jolly, listen to me. I'm leaving." My voice cracked, and I fought back tears until I could speak again. "This will be good for both of us. I promise. You'll see."

"I'm so proud of you, Holly, but I'm going to miss you so much. I already do." She pulled me into yet another hug. We'd spent the last few hours together doing some of our favorite activities while avoiding the idea that I was leaving Christmas Village, and I had no idea when I would be back. This was one goodbye I didn't want to make, but it was necessary.

"I miss you too." When the pain in my chest became too much to bear, I stepped back, giving Jolly what I hoped was a believable smile, even if it was a tad bit watery. "Be good for Mama and Papa, and stay off the Naughty List. Understand?"

"Yup, I do. Be safe, Holly."

I stepped close to her and placed a kiss to her forehead. "Always. I love you, sis."

"I love you, too."

We hugged again before joining our parents at the sleigh where I said my last goodbyes to Mama and climbed up beside Papa. There was no reason for reins since the ice dragon shifters led the way, and they were as intelligent in dragon form as they were in human form. Vixen could easily take us to New York, and that's what she did as she took off and we gained altitude. Papa and I waved to Mama and Jolly until they were little more than specks below us.

Pulling my coat tighter around my neck, I braced myself against the bitter wind blowing in my face. How did Santa do it when December was so much colder than October? The next time I saw him, I'd ask. Trying to keep my mind off those I was leaving behind, I focused instead on the business ahead.

Merric had emailed back that the "interesting" part of the cookie sheet delivery was that the company we'd bought them from had mixed up our order with someone else. We'd ended up with everything from large cookie sheets, to small cookie sheets, to cake pans, bread pans, Jell-O molds, and even a Bundt pan. I'd almost argued that we needed most of that until I'd finished reading his email: there had only been twenty each. We needed way more than twenty. Currently he was trying to track down our order and have it delivered before I arrived, but that didn't look like it was going to happen.

He'd also informed me that he'd scheduled interviews for the first two weeks of me being there. With so many elves needed, it would take that long to interview them all. Between interviews, checking on the building's progress, and settling in, it was looking to be a long and stressful few weeks. I was ever more grateful Papa would be staying for most of that time.

"You look deep in thought. Anything I can help you with?" Papa asked over the rush of the wind. He took my hand and squeezed it, trying to reassure me.

I smiled over at him. "No, I'm just trying to organize my thoughts before we arrive. This is all happening so fast, I'm not sure what to think. I don't think I'm old enough, or mature enough, but I trust you and Santa."

"And we trust you, Holly. No matter what happens, we know you'll do your best. Relax. What will happen will happen. If you can, go to sleep. We have a few hours before we land." He squeezed my hand once more before sliding down in his seat and resting his head against the top of the backrest and closed his eyes. That did not look comfortable, but he was asleep in minutes.

After spending too much time trying to find a comfortable position, I gave up, curling up on the seat so that I was sitting with my back to Papa and I could rest my head on the backrest. It wasn't any more comfortable than the previous positions, but I forced my tense muscles to loosen. The biting wind grew less severe the further South we flew, and the sleigh rocked side to side, easing me into sleep.

. . .

I COULD HAVE SWORN I'd only closed my eyes for a moment when someone was prodding me and telling me to wake up. It was Papa. Didn't he know it wasn't time to wake up? It was still dark outside. I rolled over to tell him to give me five more minutes, only to have a rude awakening when I rolled out of bed. My eyes popped open. Nope, I wasn't in bed. I'd fallen off the sleigh's bench onto the floorboards.

Several soft chuckles reached me, and my face and neck heated. I wanted nothing more than to become one with the floorboards instead of having to face those I'd embarrassed myself in front of, especially if the light, tenor voice belonged to my new assistant. This was the worst possible way to meet him. First impressions were everything, and I'd made a doozy of mine.

"You all right?" Papa asked from above me, trying to hide his laughter, though the humor in his voice gave him away.

"Yeah, I'm fine," I grumbled, sliding from the sleigh and dusting myself off before I met the eyes of those around me. Vixen stood beside Lunar in their human forms. She hid her smile behind a hand, but didn't bother to stop laughing at my expense.

My eyes swept from the two of them to the tall, blond elf standing slightly off to the side. Boy was he tall! He stood almost a foot taller than me, and I was on the taller side for elves. That had to make him just over five feet. I'd never met an elf with his height, and the rest of him...the white, button up shirt and black dress pants, they fit him just right. His grin grew even wider as my eyes widened.

I'd been staring. Full on staring. In front of him and everyone else. I must have hit my head harder than I thought, or at least that was the excuse I was going with for my less than acceptable behavior. So much for good first impressions.

"H-h-hi," I stammered, walking up to him and offering my hand. "I'm Holly. Are you Merric?"

He stared down at my hand before wrapping his much larger one around mine and shaking it. If I'd been back home, I wouldn't have bothered with a handshake, but gone straight for a hug. However, I wasn't home, and I didn't know this elf- if he was an elf. He also didn't appear to be the hugging type.

"Yes, I'm Merric. It's nice to finally meet you, Holly. Are you all right? That was quite a tumble." His boyish grin stalled my mind, and I found myself staring again until someone cleared their throat.

"Can we interrupt?" Lunar called. "The sun will be rising soon and we have to return the sleigh before sunrise."

Vix placed a hand on Lunar's chest to interject, "We'd like to say goodbye, if that's okay."

Yes, please. Save me from this humiliation. Take me with you. I so badly wanted to scream those sentiments at her, but I bit my tongue and ran to Vixen, throwing myself into her arms. These were my last goodbyes, and I didn't want to blubber in front of Merric, but why not add to the growing list of delicious gossip to spread?

"Come here, you," Lunar directed, extending his arms to me. I ran to him and threw my arms around his waist. By the time he let me go, he was wiping a few stray tears from his cheeks. "You be good, you hear? I mean it. Don't make us come back down here."

I gave him a watery smile as I laughed. "I won't. I'll be good."

"Good. Now say another farewell to Vixen while I help Chip unload your bags. Thank goodness you have less than Vixen did when we moved her out of her parent's house." Lunar winked at Vixen as he avoided her punch to his arm before jogging around the sleigh to help Papa with my things.

"So, this is it," Vix exclaimed, wrapping her arms around me. "You're going to do great. If anyone can get a bakery up and running, it's you."

"Thanks, Vix. Take care of Jolly for me, will you?"

"Of course. It should be fairly easy now that there's only one of you to keep track of."

I shook my head at her and wrapped my arms around her waist. "I love you, Vix."

"I love you too, Holly."

We held one another for several minutes, neither one of us wanting to be the first to release the other. It took Lunar clearing his throat for Vixen to step away from me. She smiled, kissed my forehead, and stepped away to shift. When Vixen shifted, I caught sight of Merric's jaw drop. Didn't he see her land? She stepped up to the sleigh and let

Lunar and Papa hook her up, all the while watching Merric. He nodded, his eyes bulging.

Too curious for my own good, and because I was who I was, I ambled over to Merric when Vixen became distracted by a question from Papa. "You look like you've never seen a dragon before."

He shook his head. "I haven't. She was already human when I made it to the roof. Wow. I've heard of the ice dragon shifters, obviously, but I've never actually seen one in person. This is amazing."

"If you think she's something to see, you should see Lunar. He's huge. Now, how do we get inside? Or did you want to watch her take off?"

His head whipped back and forth between me and Vixen. "Umm, I suppose I should take you inside. Is Chip coming?"

"He'll find his way, I'm sure. Or if you want to just tell me how to get inside, I can go by myself." The truth was that I didn't want to watch my friends leave.

Merric opened his mouth, and as he did, Papa's cell phone began to ring. My brows furrowed and every nerve I had stood on end. Papa's assistant, Dew Drop, was the only person other than me and Merric with his number, and she only called in cases of emergency when Papa was away. Not that he left too often, but sometimes he did.

Papa spoke with her, but I couldn't hear his words since he purposefully whispered into the device. My stomach squeezed. This couldn't be good. When he finished the call, Papa walked around Vixen, straight to Merric and I.

Before he spoke, he sighed, which was always a sign of bad news. "That was Christmas Village. They've had a bit of an emergency in the bakery, and I need to head back pronto. You two need to make sure this place is up and running as soon as possible. We may not have until November first after all."

"Papa, what's wrong?" I asked at the same time Merric spoke, "Chip, what happened?"

He held his hands up to slow us down. "That was Dew Drop. They've had a fire in the bakery in Christmas Village." A gasp escaped me as I threw my hands over my mouth. "I'm not sure on the extent of the damage, but no one was badly injured. Now, I need you two to do your job. Christmas isn't Christmas without cookies, is it?"

I shook my head. Merric was too stunned to move. How could there have been a fire at the bakery? Everyone was extra careful. It had never happened before in the full history of the bakery. And why now? Why did it happen now when I needed Papa the most?

Without thinking, I threw myself into his arms, not ready for this final goodbye. I'd thought I had a few weeks to build up to it, but here it was. Papa held me tight, rubbing my back.

"You've got this, baby girl. I have every confidence in you and Merric. You can do this. Now, be good." He stepped back and looked me straight in the eyes. "I mean it. Be. Good. Don't do anything mischievous that Merric will have to report back to me."

Heat filled my cheeks with Merric standing close behind us, well, within hearing of Papa's warning. "I'll be good. I promise."

"Good. Now, I need to return home. I love you." He kissed the top of my head, gave me one more farewell hug, and ran for the sleigh.

Once he was settled, Vixen extended her wings, and with a few powerful wing beats, she raced for the edge of the roof, gaining altitude before leaping over the edge. The sleigh easily missed the three foot barrier that surrounded the rooftop. Lunar ran after them, jumping from the roof and shifting in midair. Merric, who had moved closer to stand beside me, jumped when a large dragon flew straight up the side of the building where Lunar had fallen. The blast of wind from his wings sent us stumbling backward, and I reached for Merric to steady myself so that I wouldn't blow over.

Lunar soon caught up with Vixen and Papa, and they circled back as they gained altitude. I couldn't see Papa in the sleigh as they passed overhead, but I waved frantically anyway. By the time I could no longer see the tiny speck they had turned into, my muscles were screaming at me for the overuse, and my arm was like a lead weight. I let it fall to my side, but never took my gaze from the sky, even when the sleigh had long since disappeared.

I didn't realize I was crying until a soft handkerchief dabbed the tears from my cheeks. Startled, I looked to the owner of the handkerchief, my eyes wide. Merric shrugged.

"My dad always told me to be prepared with one. You never know when you'll need it, and don't worry, it's clean." He wiped the tears from my other cheek before folding the handkerchief and stuffing it back in his pocket. "I'm sorry you're hurting."

Not knowing what to say to that, I nodded and gazed back at the sky where the sleigh had disappeared, searching for some small twinkle or sign of movement that might be them. With so many lights, even this high up, there was little to see. The sleigh was gone, and so was everyone I knew.

I was now in a new city, a foreign city, surrounded by elves I'd never met, and more humans than I could possibly imagine. In fact, I'd never met a human. The realization that I would actually have a chance to meet and interact with humans stunned me. Why hadn't I thought of that before now?

"Well, do you want to go inside?" Merric set a hand on my shoulder to gain my attention.

His touch was soft and gentle, and if Jolly were here she would have teased me relentlessly the moment we were alone. The image of my sister's smiling face flashed across my mind and tears welled once again, blurring my vision. I could only nod, and he patted my back before steering me toward a small shed-like structure on one side of the roof. He opened the door, revealing a staircase leading down into the building. After waving me in to descend first, he closed the door, and I led the way into my new home.

Chapter 5

The staircase dropped us off inside the building on the top floor near an internal staircase leading down to the next floor, and next to a set of elevators. If what Papa had told me was correct, this entire floor was mine. It was huge, and I couldn't possibly use the entirety of it. Could I?

"Here, follow me." Merric led the way down a wide hall that was straight ahead. A wall with a door stood just beyond the staircase to my left, and continued down the hallway. That must have been where my apartment was located, or at least that was my guess if I remembered the floor plans correctly. This late at night I wasn't guaranteeing it, especially since Merric led us away from the door.

Construction odors filtered up the staircase, so I was glad to be leaving that area of the floor. He led me past a large room with a massive table in the center surrounded by chairs. The walls of the room were made completely of glass on three sides. Even the doors were clear, except they had our bakery's logo etched on them at eye level, well eye level for Merric.

The last wall of the room was the same dark wood paneling as the rest of the hallway and at the end of the hall we could either turn left down another hall, or we could go through the door on the right. Merric directed me to follow him through the doorway.

Inside was an office the size of my house back home. An L shaped desk at least five times larger than Papa's desk sat in the middle of the room, and file cabinets took up most of one wall. The other wall held bookcases, which were built into the wall and mostly empty. The far wall was nothing but windows. My mouth popped open, and my feet carried me across the room to enjoy the view of the city around and below me. At least the view of the lights and what I could see in the darkness.

Merric cleared his throat, and I turned back to him, my cheeks flushed. "You've never been to New York before, have you?"

"Nope. I've never left Christmas Village. This is a whole new experience. I'm a bit nervous." My cheeks flushed further until my neck heated and my hands began to sweat. I prayed he wouldn't want to randomly shake hands because the thought of him touching my sweaty hands was disgusting.

"Yeah, I bet you are. I'm sure this is nothing like Christmas Village. Now, why don't you take a few minutes and familiarize yourself with your office, and I'll go back to the roof and grab your bags and take them to your apartment. Then I'll finish the tour of the top floor." Merric grinned when I gave him a sheepish smile. How could I have forgotten my bags on the roof?

"Do you want help?"

He shook his head and strode toward the door. "Nope. You don't have much, and you're tired and I'm guessing a bit overwhelmed. Take a few minutes to take it all in and slow down. I'll be right back."

The moment he was gone, my hands flew to my hair. I was pretty sure it was a rat's nest from falling asleep in the sleigh. And my makeup, after sleeping with it on and then crying, it had to be humiliating with how awful it looked. Pushing the worry of my appearance aside, knowing there was little I could do to change it, and Merric had already seen it, I set about to explore the office as Merric had directed.

A new computer sat on one side of the wooden desk, which was color with a cherry stain. My favorite. It appeared that Papa had more influence in my office than he'd let on. Even the wooden bookcases were cherry.

The few books on the case closest to the windows caught my eye. I ran my fingertips over them as I glossed over the titles, until I reached the final book. It was an exact duplicate to the first cookie cookbook that he'd given me and Jolly for Christmas when we were small. This was a duplicate because we'd leafed through our copy so much to stare at the pages that the binding had broken and the edges were scuffed. This book had no scuffs, and I'd left our copy with Jolly. Inside were family baking recipes dating back generations, and some of my favorite cookies, muffins, cupcake decorations, and even a few pastries.

I pulled the book from the shelf and set it on my desk while continuing my appraisal of the new office. Most of the file cabinets were empty. One held blue prints, and another inventory files and recent orders. One hanging folder was stuffed with papers that I couldn't make heads or tails of what it was. I still held it when Merric found me in the office.

"What's this?" I asked, turning to find him leaning against the door frame.

"Internet bill. I'm keeping all expenditures in your office until mine is complete, that way they're organized and I don't lose anything. Is that okay?"

Shrugging, I set the paper back where I'd found it and slid the file cabinet drawer closed. "It's fine with me. There's plenty of room."

"For now. Wait until you have to make up employee files. Then it'll fill up quick."

"Employee files?" Did Papa have employee files? He hadn't mentioned any.

Merric rubbed his eyes. "Let's talk about that tomorrow. In short, every employee we hire will need a file. I'll explain specific forms tomorrow. Now, let me show you to your apartment. Then we can both go to bed. Well, one of us can go back to sleep." He chuckled as he pushed himself off the doorframe and exited the office, leaving me wishing the ground would open up and swallow me.

When it didn't, I met Merric in the hall. He continued to chuckle as he led me down the long hallway opposite my office door. This hall had wood paneling on one side and the other was the same glass windows as the office. Again, I was provided with a breathtaking view. Jolly would never believe this. Papa had agreed to give her a tablet so that we could email one another and send pictures. When I settled in, I was sending her a picture of this view, and I couldn't wait to see it in daylight.

We reached a door at the end of the hall and Merric opened it and stood back to let me enter first. Tears stung my eyes when I took in the large living room when I stepped inside. A crystal chandelier hung from a cathedral ceiling and the same floor to ceiling windows took up one wall. Two couches and a few chairs sat around a wooden coffee table. Another couch and a pair of chairs and end tables sat on the other side of the room facing a TV. The deep reds and greens warmed my heart and reminded me of home.

My bags sat near the door where Merric had left them. He stood beside them, looking rather uncomfortable while I walked further into the room. When I met his stare, he gave me a crooked grin.

"I think I should be going, unless there's something else you need from me?" When nothing came to mind, I shook my head. "All right. Sleep in and relax in the morning. After tomorrow, life will become crazy, so enjoy the free time while you have it. I took the liberty of buying some food for you. I wasn't sure what you liked, so I bought an assortment. Would you like me to give you a tour of the building tomorrow?"

I tried not to appear too eager, but my, "Yes, please" made me sound a little too desperate. Merric took it in good humor, and after confirming he'd meet me at noon, he left me alone to explore the rest of the apartment.

Beyond the living room was a hallway that I assumed led to the bedroom, but I skipped it and headed in search of the kitchen. After the night I'd had, I was in need of a strong cup of hot chocolate. The kitchen was as amazing as the living room and my office. Every appliance was high tech and clean. In fact, the entire room was spotless. My first task was to raid the cupboards to find the hot chocolate mix, and when I came up empty, I searched again. When that search was as fruitless as the first, I began tapping my foot in annoyance. How could an elf forget the one major food ingredient of Christmas? Unless I couldn't find it, but where else would he put it? Yes, he'd picked up an assortment of tasty foods, but that wasn't what I needed.

Heading into the living room, I pulled my tablet out of my backpack and opened the email app. This late at night he wouldn't be checking his email- in fact he was probably asleep by now- but I needed to find out where it was for breakfast. After sending a quick message that I hoped he'd find early in the morning, I decided to move on from the kitchen and take my belongings to the bedroom.

I shouldn't have been surprised that there was more than one bedroom in the apartment, but three was a bit excessive in my opinion. After all, why would I need three bedrooms? Two of the bedrooms shared a bathroom located in the hallway, and the third, the Master Bedroom, had its own private bath. Without a doubt, that was the one I claimed as mine.

The King sized bed with its plush comforter called to me and I wanted nothing more than to drop my load of belongings and dive under the sheets. I had a bit more sense than that. I set everything down gently and then dove onto the bed. The soft mattress and bedspread threatened to swallow me whole, and I willingly let it. I didn't remember closing my eyes, but I must have.

It wasn't for long. A soft, yet high pitched ding woke me, and I wasn't sure how long it had been since my eyes closed. Another ding followed it, and I sat up to find my tablet, nearly falling over from lingering sleep. My eyes widened and sleep left me when I saw the dinging was sounding because of emails from Merric.

"You won't find any. I may have forgotten to buy hot chocolate mix. I'm sorry about that. It slipped my mind."

And the second email: "I'll purchase some for you first thing in the morning. Again, my apologies."

My brain didn't know whether to be appalled that an elf had forgotten to buy hot chocolate or giddy that he would be bringing me some. The weird concoction of emotions didn't help my response any. In fact, it left me sounding stupid, but it was almost two in the morning, so it couldn't be helped.

"Thanks, I appreciate it."

I hit send and wished I'd said something a little more… A little more what? It was time for bed. My brain was leaving me behind and I could no longer be responsible for what came out of my mouth or what my fingers typed, or didn't type. Instead of analyzing my response any further, I tossed the tablet onto a side chair, changed into pajamas, and slid under the covers. I planned to do exactly what Merric suggested and sleep in.

. . .

A BUZZING SOUND pulled me from my dreams, and when it stopped, I moaned and clung tighter to my pillow. Then the buzzer came again. And again. Knowing that it came from the front of the apartment, I threw a sweatshirt over my pajamas and shuffled out to the living room where the buzzer met me even louder.

The apartment door. That was great. I ran my hands through my hair and my fingers under my eyes to make myself look partially presentable and opened the door. A startled Merric stood on the other side, fully dressed again in a button up white shirt and black dress pants. Even his shoes were shiny. As if to explain why he was there, he held out a large box of hot chocolate mix.

"It's ten o'clock. I thought you'd be awake."

"It doesn't feel like ten o'clock," I mumbled, taking the box from him. A small smile quirked at the corners of his mouth. "And you're telling me you went to bed after two this morning and went shopping already?"

"Yes. I emailed asking if I'd forgotten anything else, but you never responded. I see why. Well, I'll let you go back to bed or whatever you want to do. I'll see you in a few hours. Unless you want to postpone your tour?"

Shaking my head, I hid a yawn behind my hand. "Nope, I'm good. I'm awake. I'll see you in a few hours."

He nodded and strode down the hall. After closing my door, I let my head thud against it. I probably looked as horrendous as the Grinch. Merric would likely be having nightmares for weeks after this interaction.

I dropped the box on the kitchen island and headed straight for the shower without bothering to look at my reflection. There was no way I wanted to know what he saw. When my eyes fell on the bathtub that was complete with jets, I almost changed my mind from showering to a bath, but I needed to be quick. Two hours was plenty of time to be ready for the day, but I preferred to be early, and after I'd scarred Merric already, I wanted to redeem myself. Plus, I was still living out of a suitcase. It would take a bit longer to find an outfit.

After cleaning up for the day, I finally took the chance to study my room. It had the same color scheme as the living room, and the furniture was a spotless black. Another TV sat on a dresser, complete with DVD player. Since I didn't have any movies, that feature would go unused for a while. Plus, I would probably be too tired and too busy to watch movies for a while.

It was almost noon when my first cup of hot chocolate was brewed to perfection, or as close as it could come in New York. Merric had done his best, but there was no way anyone could top the homemade mixes that elves put together in Christmas Village. However much I may not have liked the taste as opposed to back home, I would never mention it to Merric. I appreciated the thoughtfulness and consideration he'd shown in purchasing some early this morning.

At one minute to noon, the buzzer rang. At least Merric was prompt, yet not too early. That was a blessed relief.

"Hi, come on in." I ushered Merric inside after answering the door and he stepped inside with some hesitation. When he finally looked at me carefully, his boyish smirk grew.

"Good morning again. You do realize you have a hot chocolate mustache, right?"

I what?

Leaving Merric standing by the door, I covered my mouth and raced to my bathroom. Sure enough, a thin hot chocolate line covered the skin just above my upper lip. Groaning as loud as I dared with Merric in the apartment, I wiped up the sticky residue and debated locking myself in my room for the day. At this point, he was probably wondering why Papa and Santa had chosen me. I knew I was.

Merric was standing beside the wall with the huge windows with his back to me when I finally decided I could face him again. His hands were deep in his pockets, and he appeared relaxed. Again, I couldn't help but notice how tall he was. His short, blond hair was mussed so it stood up from his scalp like dozens of tiny spikes, and the blond of it accented the tan of his skin. I'd never been tan in my life. North Pole weather didn't exactly make that a plausible experience.

"I'm sorry about that," I commented, and he jumped a little when I spoke.

He turned to me with a smile and shrugged. "That's all right. Are you ready now?"

Wringing my hands, I made my way toward the door where he joined me. "I'm going to say yes. I suppose we'll find out soon enough if I'm ready."

"Yeah, I suppose you're right. Okay, follow me."

Chapter 6

Numbers on a paper meant little to me when staring at blue prints. Actually walking the building? That gave me the real information I needed for how large the space was. Now that I was better rested, I could more easily see how large and expansive my floor was. Besides my apartment, office, and conference room, they had built me my own personal gym and an in-home theater. Merric hadn't picked out any movies since he wasn't sure what I liked, but told me if I let him know, he'd buy them for me.

"You really don't have to do that," I told him as we rode the elevator to the basement floors.

"I'm your assistant, Holly. If you need something, all you have to do is ask."

Biting my lip, I shook my head. "I thought we were more like partners in this. You run one side and I run the other. You know, financials and bakery."

"Yes, that's how it is split, but in the true scheme of this production, you're going to be far more important, which means it's my job to assist and make sure you have what you need. Truly, Holly, if there is ever anything that you need, please tell me. Or even if there's something that you want, let me know. I will do what I can to make it happen."

By the time we reached the lowest level, I still wasn't sure how I felt about this arrangement. I still couldn't see how I was the one with the harder job. Running a bakery wouldn't be that hard, would it? At least Papa always made it look so easy.

The elevator came to a halt, and I grabbed the hand rail that wrapped around the inside. Merric was a gentleman and didn't comment on my weird reaction. I'd watched human movies with elevators, but since Christmas Village didn't have any, I had never ridden in one. This was another experience I'd have to share with Jolly. She was going to be beyond jealous, and I couldn't wait.

"So this level is where we keep janitorial supplies and other equipment for storage. Spare baking supplies are over there," he pointed to the far left corner before swinging his arm to the right, "and extra office supplies are there. There's not much to see on this level. I have paper documents that show how much extra we have, which will be easier to see than going through it down here."

"For now that will work," I told him, nodding as we stepped back into the elevator, and I gripped the handrail. "After we start up I'll want the extra inventoried at least monthly to make sure we don't run low. Extra is only good if you keep enough in stock."

The elevator doors closed as Merric pulled a cell phone from his pocket. "I'll make a note of that and make sure someone is assigned to do that."

"You have a cell phone?"

"Yup, and you do too. It's in one of your desk drawers. I put it there for safe keeping. Sorry, I meant to tell you about it last night, but it slipped my mind."

The elevator slowed and the doors opened. "That's okay. We were both tired, and I wouldn't have remembered anything you told me about it anyway. Wow."

Row upon row of shelving lined a single walkway down the center of this level and extended across the entire building. Crates and pallets littered the ground and boxes sat on shelves. If I hadn't realized before how massive this project was, I did now. This was the dry foods floor. According to Merric, the fridges and freezers were on the next floor up. Sudden panic caused my heart to skip and a few shallow gasps escaped me.

"Are you all right?" Merric stepped close to me and placed a hand on my forehead. "You went as pale as a sheet and you're breathing wrong. Do you need to sit? Lay down?"

"I'm fine." I shook my head, dislodging his hand from my skin. "A little overwhelmed. It's one thing to see all of this on paper. It's another to see it in person and know I'm responsible for making this happen. I don't want to fail Papa or Santa, but I'm not sure I can do this."

"Yes, you can." His voice was firm and his gaze steady as he looked down on me. "They would not have chosen you if they didn't think you could do it, and you're not alone. I'm here to help, even if that help is to bring you hot chocolate in the morning, or even in the middle of the night. Now, breathe. We're taking this one step at a time."

My breathing normalized, but my stomach still twisted. Merric refused to look away until I nodded at him. "Thanks." A grin curved my lips. "I'll try not to want more hot chocolate in the middle of the night, but you should know that what you bought me won't last long."

He closed his eyes and groaned. "I was afraid of that. I'll make it a top priority to buy more. If you can make a list of other food you need, I'll make sure to grab those items too."

"Merric, this is insane. You're going to burn yourself out keeping up with me and going on grocery runs."

"At first, maybe, but we'll figure it out, and once we have a routine set up, it'll be easier."

Shaking my head, I headed down the aisle, taking mental inventory of what was stored here. Well, that was the attempt. Instead of focusing on flour, sugar, and other baking essentials, my brain was too busy trying to figure Merric out. Was he really the best assistant anyone could dream of having? And did he actually sleep?

"So, how long has this project been in place?" If I wanted to know more, I had to ask the right questions. Hopefully this line of questioning would lead to fruitful information. Interrogations had never been my strong suite. That was all Jolly.

Merric entered an aisle and crouched to investigate a damaged crate. Satisfied there was no internal damage, he rejoined me. "The building was purchased over a year ago, but no one knew when it would begin use as a bakery. After last Christmas, Santa and your father sat down and looked at the numbers and decided to push the project ahead. That's when they called me in to start handling the remodel and managing the project."

"So…I'm kind of stepping on your toes by taking over the project and having you as my assistant." Was he trying to kill me with kindness or biding his time to seek revenge?

His chuckle echoed in the spacious room. "No, you are most certainly not stepping on my toes. This is a bakery. I'm a numbers guy. I know that half a cup plus half a cup equals one cup, but you have me put anything in those cups and make it turn into something edible and I'm lost. Once this place starts to function as an actual bakery, your skills will far surpass mine."

"Maybe," I muttered.

"Time will tell," he confirmed, stopping as we reached the opposite end of the room. "Now, we can either walk back to the elevator or we could take the stairs up to the next level."

"Stairs. I love stairs. More than that elevator anyway."

"You say that now, but after a long day and you're on this floor, you'll be happy to ride that elevator to your floor."

"Maybe. Lead the way."

He did, and we toured the next level, which was about as productive as walking the level below. It would be far easier to check on our supplies via a sheet of paper instead of counting down there. We were going to need a team of elves to keep that inventory accurate.

We'd just made our way to the main floor when my tablet registered an email. I pulled up the app as I waited for Merric to speak to our oven installers, who had met us on this floor. The email was from Papa, and my stomach dipped as I read.

"Hello Holly, I hope your first day is going well for you. We miss you, especially Jolly. She's moping around the house. I keep telling her to find a different job, but she's dragging her feet. And about that, we've had to reassign most of the bakers to different jobs. The damage to the bakery was far more extensive than I first thought it was when Dew Drop called me. We will be out of commission this Christmas season making the repairs. I hate to put any more pressure on you, but you're our only hope for Christmas cookie distribution. It's already affecting the elves here in Christmas Village. As far as I can remember, we've never ran out of cookies and other baked goods before. When you get up and running, we'd appreciate it if you could send us what you can spare from your other human orders. We should be back online and functional by next year, but it will be too late for this season. I love you, Holly. If there's anything you need, please let me know, or tell Merric. He's there to take as much pressure off of you as he can. Good luck with the interviews. Be sure to ask them if they know the difference between granulated sugar and powdered sugar. If they don't know there's a difference, do not allow them to touch an oven. All my love, Papa."

I closed the email and walked away from where Merric and the man were in a heated discussion. It would be my luck that we'd hit another snag and would be further behind. Since we were on the first floor, I could see out the windows at street level. These windows were darker, and Merric had explained that they were tinted. Since most of this level was for greeting potential clients and other humans who may be curious about us, it held mostly desks and private rooms. I doubted most would ever be used, but they hadn't wanted to place any ovens on this level.

"I hope that was good news," I warned Merric when he joined me to stare out the window. His breathing was in short, sharp breaths and his jaw was clenched. Not a good sign.

He sighed and rubbed his neck. "No, it wasn't. The company that was sending the ovens just contacted our installer to tell him half of the ovens we're waiting on have been backordered."

"What does that mean?"

"It means they're out of stock and when they get more then they'll ship them to us. The new ship date is the middle of November."

Fighting the urge to sit down and cry, I turned and leaned against the glass wall and stared out across the expansive room. "Okay, how many do we have installed right now?"

"Half. The next quarter will be delivered and in place by the end of the week. That still leaves the quarter we'll need unaccounted for." He rubbed his face and ran his fingers through his spiked hair, leaving the spikes oddly bent instead of standing straight.

Holding the tablet to my chest, I tapped it as I thought and paced a small circle near where we stood. This was bad, but it could have been worse, though I would never say that out loud. Papa had always told me to keep thoughts like that to myself, and right now I would listen to any and all of his wisdom.

"Okay, so we know we're short ovens, but that's okay. We can make it work. If we can have them installed by the end of November and in use, then we can still make the December rush. We'll also be making less for elves to eat and saving more for human orders, which will help at first."

Merric nodded. "It could work. If Chip says they can stay operational, then that would be better." My grimace caught his attention and his eyes narrowed. "What?"

"Papa emailed and I just read it. The damage was extensive. They won't be operational until after Christmas."

Growling, Merric leaned against the window and slid to the floor, much as I'd longed to do after reading the email. I hadn't wanted him to view it as defeat or weakness on my part, but it appeared he didn't see it that way, nor did he care. After all, he was the one sitting on a dirty floor wearing black pants. Every speck of dirt and dust would cling to those pants.

"Are you giving up?" That wasn't the type of person I gauged him to be, especially after he'd woken up early to bring me hot chocolate mix.

"No, just momentarily defeated. I will not wave a flag of surrender until every ounce of flour is gone, every oven is out of order, and every elf has gone on strike. I need a moment to gather my thoughts and then I'll be fine. Are you giving up?"

A giggle burst from me, which earned me an arched eyebrow stare. "Merric, I haven't even started yet. I'm not giving up. Papa didn't just send me down here for my baking skills. You've never seen me in a snowball fight before. I don't give up, and when I have to, I play dirty. This is going to happen, and if we have to bend a few rules along the way, so be it."

He grinned up at me. It was a devilish grin that matched mine and had heat flooding my veins. "I like the way you think, Holly."

"You say that now. You may find yourself regretting it later."

"If it pushes us through this challenge, I won't regret it. Afterward, that's a possibility. Now, let's finish this tour and then we can discuss a more detailed plan of attack, which includes questions for the interviews. There are obviously normal questions everyone asks, but you'll want your own, I'm sure."

"Yup, and Papa made sure to remind me to ask them if they know the difference between granulated sugar and powdered sugar."

"Isn't sugar just sugar?"

"And that's why you're not a baker. Here, take my hand and I'll help you up."

Merric swatted my hand away and stood on his own. "Thanks for the offer, but I think you'd be down here with me and we'd be a pile of knees and elbows if you tried to help."

"That's true, you are tall for an elf." And not for the first time I wondered how that could be, but he shrugged it off.

"Have you eaten lunch?" He stared at my stomach as it gave a low, long rumble.

"Um, no. I had hot chocolate for breakfast, well, brunch, I guess."

"You don't happen to have any clothes that are less...Christmasy, do you?" He motioned to my outfit, which consisted of dark green pants and a red and white polka dot shirt. It was long sleeved and the warmer temperatures were heating me up, but I'd never worn short sleeves. The North Pole weather had never allowed it.

"This is what I have, Merric. Why?"

He shifted his weight and his eyes swept between me and the exit. Was he planning to run? His unease ushered self doubt to take a front row seat in my brain. He wore a white shirt and black pants to fit in with the other business people walking along the street. I focused on the women. Most business types wore pantsuits or skirts with jackets, and most were in plain, darker colors. However, there were several others who wore various styles, but none of them were anywhere near Christmas colors.

"Merric, it's not like I'm wearing a sweatshirt with a picture of a Christmas tree or Santa on the front of it."

Ignoring my remark, he smirked at me. "You want to grab a New York City hot dog from a street vendor? You can't be here without eating one."

Chapter 7

I soon learned that it wasn't my outfit which had Merric nervous to take me outside, but the weather. We were two blocks from the bakery when the skies opened up and the rain descended. For it being the beginning of October, the raindrops were cold. Merric grabbed me and pulled me under a store's entrance overhang, but it was already too late. The gusher had soaked us.

My shirt was thick, which prevented the white polka dots from being see through, unlike Merric's thin, white button up. Water dripped from his head onto his shirt, and wherever wasn't already wet, soaked up the new water. I was about to thank him from saving me from drowning when the wind blew, forcing the rain to blow under the overhang in a torrential downpour that left me gasping until Merric stepped in front of me, blocking the water.

"Go inside!" Merric yelled above the storm as humans ran past us on the sidewalk and others shoved their way into the store to avoid the onslaught.

I did as he directed, squeezing between people that Merric had pointed out earlier were tourists, and he snuck in with others. When I cleared the space in front of the door, I veered right to find a less occupied section of the large clothing store. My companion joined me seconds later, more drenched than he'd looked before the wind gust.

"We may have to buy a towel," I told him, using my hand to wipe some rainwater droplets from his cheeks, but more streamed down from the top of his head to replace them. "You're soaking wet."

"I'm going to need more than a towel," he muttered, staring down at his shirt. My eyes followed his and I had to swallow hard. His shirt stuck to his skin, so I could tell he wasn't the most heavily built man alive, but he had more muscle than I did. However, even without pounds of muscle, the muscle he did have was toned, and I'd never seen any man, in person or on TV, who looked better in a wet shirt that could have been a second skin.

His eyes lifted, and he caught me staring. Heat ballooned all over my body and I knew without a doubt my face was redder than the shirt I wore. How stupid could I have been to stare? At least he had the decency not to smirk, but he gave me his boyish grin.

"I knew I should have grabbed my umbrella. Would you mind if we skipped the hotdog today?"

I'd never wanted to hug a man more in my life. He'd saved me from complete humiliation with utter dignity. Papa had chosen an excellent assistant.

"Are the hotdogs leaving the city?"

"No."

"Then we can eat them another day. If we both don't change out of these wet clothes, we'll get sick, and we don't have time for that. Do we?"

"No, ma'am."

Ma'am? He'd just called me ma'am? No one had ever called me that. I brushed it off and faced the window, watching the rain continue in blowing waves.

"Should we stay here until it's over or make a run for it?"

He pulled his phone from his pocket and tapped a few buttons. Now I was even more glad he'd suggested I leave my tablet in one of the locked rooms on the bakery's main floor. It was brand new and I didn't want it ruined already.

"This storm is going to last a while, and heavier rain is behind this. Either we stay and look around, or we run. Since we're-I'm- already soaked, we might as well make a run for it. We can change and I'll order in pizza for you. What kind would you like?"

Giggling at the idea of running through my first real rain storm that didn't include ice, I responded, "Surprise me."

"I can do that. Let's go."

He took my hand and led me back toward the door. The tourists were taking the time to shop while the storm rained itself out. We didn't have time to waste, and as Merric led us through the door, I braced myself for the cool water.

It hit in a strong wave, and I squealed and giggled as it hit me. Merric's tinkling tenor laugh reached me over the gusting of the wind seconds before he ran with me down the street. Our connected hands allowed him to keep track of me as he led us up the sidewalk, racing across intersections where the orange stop hand was clearly telling us not to cross.

When we arrived at our building, I was breathless, both from the run and laughter. He pulled us inside, snickering at me. One of the oven installers was on his cell phone in the main lobby and watched us cracking up with a look of annoyance. His phone call while my ovens still weren't ready to use wasn't worth me being quiet in the echoing room.

"That was fun," I told my assistant as he shook his head like I'd seen dogs do on TV.

"Fun, sure, and wet. Very wet. Well, I'm going to the building next door and change. You should go to your apartment and change as well. I'll order the pizza. Hopefully by the time they deliver it, the rain will have let up a bit. I don't like soggy pizza." He again produced his phone and punched a few buttons.

"It's good pizza?"

Merric peered up from his phone to give me a narrow-eyed stare. "You aren't a pizza snob, are you?"

"No. Honestly I doubt I would know good or bad pizza from what you order. I've never had pizza before. The dragons prefer steaks and we elves preferred all things sugar. If we had a meal with lots of meat, it was usually hamburgers and the occasional steak."

He blinked at me, hit a button on his phone, and raised it to his ear. "Hey, yeah, it's me. I need a large of my usuals. Nope, larges. Thanks." When he ended the call, still wearing a dumbfounded expression, he crossed his arms and studied me. "A friend of mine owns a pizza joint. His pizza is excellent, and even if it were only passable, I'd still consider it amazing because he doesn't charge me a delivery fee. Now, it'll be a half an hour. That's plenty of time for you to change into something dry, as well as me. When the pizza arrives, I'll bring it up. We can eat in your office, if you'd like. That would allow us to go over more business details. Okay?"

I nodded and bid him farewell. He turned to the door and I headed toward the elevator, ready to be rid of my wet things. The ride up wasn't nearly as daunting as the descent had been. When I stepped out, empty halls greeted me. A pang of loneliness hit my heart. Besides sleeping and cleaning up for the day, Merric had been by my side since I'd gotten here.

Pushing back all thought except to change into dry clothes, I headed toward my apartment. I needed to unpack my clothes anyway, so I might as well use my time to do that as well. If we had to wait a half an hour, I could make a good start in turning my large apartment into my new home.

Twenty minutes later I'd changed into dry clothes and had unpacked all of my belongings. Since I hadn't brought much with me besides clothes, it hadn't been a long process. With extra time on my hands, I made a mug of hot chocolate and strode to my office, hoping Merric would see the open door and find me there.

The book Papa had given me still lay on my desk. There was no doubt in my mind it came from him. Who else would have a copy of this book? I sat behind the desk, set my mug down, and flipped open the book to a random page in the middle. A recipe I had made a few times jumped off the page and I delved into it, already knowing its ingredients, but after so much time had passed without making it, I'd become rusty on the quantities.

I'd lost myself in the book, reading recipe after recipe, when two boxes of pizza slid across my desk, nearly bumping into the book. Glancing up, still blurry eyed from reading, I found Merric standing on the other side of the desk.

"I see you found the special book your father requested I leave in your office. He told me it wouldn't take you long to notice it."

After flipping the book closed, I pushed it off to the side so it would be out of the way and wouldn't have pizza splatter all over it. I'd heard pizza was greasy, and I didn't want that grease anywhere near my dearest possession here. When the lid was lifted off the first box, I was happy I'd moved the book away.

"That smells amazing." I leaned over the box, taking in a deep breath that caused my stomach to rumble. When it began an encore performance, Merric picked up a slice of pizza and shoved it at me.

"Eat, or Chip will think I'm neglecting my duty to assist you and keep you taken care of properly. He can probably hear your stomach growling all the way to the North Pole."

Rolling my eyes, I stuck the pizza in my mouth and bit down. "Oh my gosh, this is amazing," I spoke with my mouth full of pizza and my eyes wide with astonishment. The flavors bursting in my mouth weren't like any other flavor combination I'd ever experienced. Who knew cheese could be that stringy and delicious?

"I told you it was the best. You should never doubt me."

"I will never doubt you again, my friend."

"Good. Now let's work and eat. Then I'll give you the final tour of the baking floors, and then I'll let you have the evening off. It may be the last relaxing evening you have for a while."

I took another bite and motioned him to sit in a chair across the desk from me. He pulled it up to the desk and set a notepad and pen next to the pizza boxes and grabbed a slice. When I glanced at the notebook and arched an eyebrow at him, he chuckled.

"Greasy fingers and technology don't mix well." With that he lifted the pen and we went to work making notes of items we still needed to take care of and interview questions.

IT WAS late evening by the time we finished the tour of three baking floors. They'd started installing ovens and other necessary equipment on the lower levels and worked their way up. That meant there was at least two floors below my office that would not be used until the middle of November. All in all, the setup of each floor was organized and much like that of Christmas Village.

A store room held dry and wet ingredients which the head baker on that floor would be in charge of dispersing and keeping organized. Multiple stations around the room were set up as their own unique baking area, and each area had every baking utensil and other supplies they would need, or could possibly need, in cabinets and drawers along the outer wall that were connected to that station's ovens.

The center of the room held tables for cooling racks and decorating areas for cakes and cookies. The separate area would allow others to decorate while the initial bakers continued on to the next batches. Other stations around the room would serve to help alleviate stress from everyone else.

"So, Chip explained that at Christmas Village each floor has a different flavor of whatever you're making," Merric stated as he walked me to my room. "I know that's the goal here, but with some of the floors still not in operation, I think for now we might want to double up some of the floors."

I stopped to stare out at the city, at least what I could see of it through the rain and fog. "Yeah, I think you're right. Do we have some say in what cookies we make?"

Merric smirked. "You're in charge of this operation. What do you say?"

"You mean Papa didn't give any direction about that?"

"He's trying to leave as much of the decision making as he can to you. Why? Did you have something in mind?"

"Well, maybe. I mean, we have to make sure all of the traditional cookies are made, but if we have space and time, there are a few others I'd like to add to the mix."

He nodded, joining me at the window. "That could work. We may have to wait and see how quickly we can produce what we have to, but I think with some luck we can add a few others."

"Thanks."

"Don't thank me," he replied, shaking his head. "This is your operation. I'm just here to help you out."

"And that's why I'm thanking you. It's nice to have someone to bounce ideas off of who sees the same picture I do. Well, I'd better go find something to eat."

"You mean you want more hot chocolate."

My cheeks heated at his teasing. Jolly would have called me out on it, so I was ever more thankful she wasn't around. No wonder I'd never been asked out on a date, not that I was dating my assistant, or had any intention of doing so. It was just nice to react to a man and not have it mentioned in front of him. Jolly always meant well, but the results weren't great.

"Yeah, I'm dying for a cup. Do you want some?" I asked, almost as an afterthought.

He shook his head and moved to leave. "No, I'm not a big hot chocolate drinker. It's nice, but I prefer straight, cold milk."

"With cookies?"

"Cake."

My giggle echoed up and down the hall. "Well, at least you have a sweet tooth."

"Yes, I did inherit my mother's sweet tooth." He hesitated and then shrugged. "She has the biggest sweet tooth of anyone I know, but I have a feeling she's met her match in you."

"That may be a possibility."

Merric waved and started back down the hall since we were practically at my door. "Have your hot cocoa and go to bed. And set an alarm. We meet at seven thirty in the conference room for interview prep. And that's seven thirty in the morning," he yelled back, disappearing around the corner.

Yeah, he did not buy me enough hot chocolate mix if he wanted me to be ready to interview elves that early every morning for the next two weeks. We had well over one hundred elves to interview, and we had to hire most, just not all of them would be bakers. After all, someone had to take inventory and keep the building clean and working properly.

"When did I become an adult?" The question hung in the air unanswered as I stepped into my apartment and headed for the kitchen and a box of hot chocolate mix.

Chapter 8

"Papa, can you let Jolly read the below letter? Thanks."

I stared at the tablet screen, unsure of what to say. I'd never gone this long without seeing my twin, let alone not speaking to her. Since I hadn't heard from her yet, I wasn't sure if Papa had gotten around to giving her a tablet with email access yet. He had as much happening back home as I had here, so the chances were unlikely she had a private email account yet. Since this message was monitored, I didn't want to be as frank and honest about how I wasn't sure of what I was doing, and how my hands were shaking just thinking about the interviews I was about to conduct with Merric within the hour. At least having the email monitored meant I didn't have to say a thing about my new assistant. Jolly would understand… and grill me that much more later.

"Jolly, I hope you're doing great! Have you finally chosen a new job yet? If not, I'm requesting Mama sign you up for voluntary snow removal duty. I miss you! Life is good here. A bit stressful at the moment. I'm about to start interviewing elves for the open positions."

Merric walked into the conference room with a cardboard box in his hands that he set on the table and slid to me. The scent of hot cocoa, cookies, and muffins escaped their containers to reach my nose. A contented sigh escaped me and I closed my eyes to bask in the scent. I'd eaten a small bowl of cereal for breakfast, but it hadn't been nearly as satisfying as the food now sitting next to me.

"Jolly, I have to go. Time to start. Talk later. Love you." I finished typing out my letter and sent it while Merric emptied the box on the table beside me to reveal four to-go cups of hot chocolate, a container of bakery chocolate chip cookies and another of assorted muffins.

"I wasn't sure what you liked, so I decided to give you a variety." He sat in the chair beside me, notepad and pen in hand. They had also appeared out of the box with the food. Our list of questions was on the first sheet, which he tore out of the notebook and lay on the table between us for reference. "Today is going to be a long day, so I thought I'd start us off on the right foot."

"You may be my favorite person in the world right now," I told him before taking a bite of a poppy seed muffin.

We took the final minutes before the first interview to finish discussing questions and how the interviews would work. To save time, Merric had scheduled some husbands and wives to interview together. He again reminded me that these interviews were less about hiring or not hiring elves, but seeing where they would fit best. They were all aware that the majority of the positions available were for bakery staff.

Our first interviewee was right on time, and my eyes bugged out when I saw her step off the elevators through the glass walls. She was dressed in a dark beige skirt, black top, and suit jacket that matched her skirt. It was nothing like what I'd seen an elf wear before. I'd thought Merric's clothes odd, but this elf took the cake in her spiky heels.

Merric stood and opened the conference room door for the elf and ushered her inside. "Hi, I'm Liz." She shoved her hand at him, and he accepted it gracefully. "You must be Merric, the elf who sent out the job notice."

"Yes, and this is Holly." He motioned to me, and I stood to meet her. How did she move so quick in those shoes without breaking an ankle? I loved my red and green sneakers. They were practical, comfortable, and safe.

"It's nice to meet you," I told Liz, shaking her hand.

"You as well. So, you're the one in charge?"

"Yes. Please, have a seat." I motioned to the open chair across from where Merric and I were seated. He joined me while Liz took her seat. After sitting, I wiped my hands on my pants to remove the sweat and hide their trembling.

"So, which position are you interested in, Liz?" Merric asked, resting his arms on the table. If he was nervous, he didn't show it. He spewed confidence and appeared far too comfortable.

She sat straight, her gaze hopping between the two of us. "Well, I would love an administrative position, but I noticed that none were listed. If there isn't one available, I suppose a baking position would be best."

"Liz, how do you feel about humans?" I asked her, which caused Merric to glance at me in surprise. That wasn't a question we'd prepared. In fact, it had slipped off my tongue before I could filter the question.

The other woman shifted slightly, but kept her focus, obviously not expecting this question either. "Well, I like humans. After all, we share the planet and celebrate together. I would never date one, but I have several human friends who I'm close with."

"Okay. Thanks. That's all the questions we have. If we need more information, we'll be in contact."

Merric's eyebrows shot up and Liz let out a small, "Oh." I stood to show the interview was over. The other two followed my example as I strode around the table and walked Liz to the door. Giving her a warm smile, I bid her farewell and watched as her and her heels made their way to the elevator.

"You want to explain that?" Merric asked after I'd shut the conference room door.

"Front lobby receptionist. There's no way those manicured fingers, that suit, and those heels are going anywhere near baked goods. Plus, she's the epitome of business woman. She can help us make a great first impression."

He cocked his head to the side, thinking. "And that's why you asked how she felt about humans?"

"Yup. If she has human friends, then she's comfortable around humans. Not all elves are. Did you see the way they stared at me yesterday?"

"I ignored the stares. Now, we have a bit of time before the next interview."

Sitting back down, I took a swig of hot chocolate from the second cup. I needed to hurry. They were beginning to cool off more than I liked. After swallowing, I watched Merric make a note on his pad, and tension settled in the pit of my stomach.

"Merric, was it okay that I ended the interview like that? I should have consulted you on it, and not made the decision of where to put her on my own. I'm sorry."

He looked up at me, a small frown turning his lips down. I played with the lid of my cup to avoid his gaze. Since I hadn't been here long, we hadn't had much time to work together, and certainly hadn't annoyed the other or made them upset yet. It was quite possible I'd done that now. Usually when I upset someone, it didn't bother me too much. Maybe because I had Jolly right there with me, and she had the bigger mouth. However, that I'd upset Merric bothered me more than I was ready to admit.

"You did what you thought was best. I would have liked to ask her a few more questions, but you saw what I didn't. Like I said, when it comes to baking, I'll trust your opinion." His words were measured, which didn't make me relax and feel any better. If anything, I felt worse.

My eyes started to sting, and panic set in. I couldn't cry. I never cried, well not until I'd had to say goodbye to my family. Why was I about to cry now?

"Excuse me. I'll be right back." I grabbed my tablet and escaped the room before Merric could ask what was wrong, show concern, or register the next wave of shock I caught on his face when I fled my chair.

In the safety of my office, I closed the door and paced the room. If I had been thinking, I would have brought one of the hot chocolate cups with me. What was wrong? He was right, I'd done what I thought was best. This was my project, and he was the assistant, even if I was seeing him more as a friend than assistant.

The reason for my weird mood hit me as a soft knock echoed off my door. After hearing that knock the last two days, I'd know it anywhere. He didn't want to disturb me, but he wanted me to answer. Taking a deep breath to steady my nerves, I walked to the door and turned the knob.

Merric stood with his arms crossed on the other side, his eyes bright with concern. "Did I say something? I feel like I upset you. That wasn't my intention."

"It wasn't mine to upset you in the conference room. I'm sorry for how the interview went." I bit my tongue to make it stop talking as his eyebrows furrowed.

"You didn't upset me. Surprised, yes, but not upset." He rubbed his brow as he spoke. "I tend to frown and look mad when I'm thinking. I was trying to see what you saw in her. I thought it might help in later interviews to see what you're looking for."

"Oh."

"What's wrong, Holly? There's more to this than that interview, isn't there? Or am I seeing something that isn't there?"

"It's so quiet around here. How can you stand it? Where's the Christmas music?" I asked Merric, longing filling my voice.

He shook his head at me, and I could tell he fought not to roll his eyes. "We don't play music."

"Well, that needs to change. This is the gloomiest building I've ever been in. Our bakery's name is The Christmas Village Bakery, so let's make it fit the name. Santa would be appalled if he stepped foot in this building. A little tinsel and lights never killed anybody. Add decorators to your list of jobs. This place needs to live up to its name."

"But it's October. You want Christmas decorations up now?"

I studied his face for several seconds, registering the surprise and uncertainty in his eyes. Papa had always said that elves who didn't live at Christmas Village were different, but I'd never asked how, and now I was seeing it. They just didn't love Christmas like the rest of us.

"Yes, I want decorations up now. Lots of them. And I want music. I want lights. I want snow."

His eyebrows rose halfway up his forehead. "Snow? Now that I don't think I can do."

"Okay, fine, take snow off the list."

"Holly, with everything else going on and barely going to be making this deadline, why are you so adamant to have decorations put up? I don't understand."

"Because I'm homesick!" I cried. Frustration filled me and tears slipped from my eyes. "I'm from Christmas Village, Merric. We do Christmas every day of the year. Every. Single. Day. There's lights, music, snowball fights, toys, pine trees, garland, choirs, and so much more I can't even describe it. Yes, this city is beautiful, but everywhere I turn it's one wall after another. There's no color, and it's so quiet."

Turning away to hide my tears, I walked to the desk and opened the only piece of home that I had with me. Papa had known I would need this. The tears wanted to fall faster, but I refused to let them. Instead, I cleared my head, refusing to think of home. We were too busy for me to have a meltdown. I could do that later, in private.

A throat cleared behind me, and I flushed, too humiliated by my outburst to turn around. "Holly, I'm sorry. I forget about the differences between your home and here. Maybe if I'd been to Christmas Village before I would understand how you must feel. I will do what I can to make this place more like home for you, but it will take some time."

"You don't have to," I told him, turning around to give him a watery smile. "You were right. We've got too much happening to bother with decorations, and it's all far more important."

"No, you're right," Merric argued. "We're making Christmas cookies. We should have something that reminds us of that. Otherwise we're just bakers and just another bakery. After all, like you said, this is The Christmas Village Bakery. Now, our next interviewee should be here any minute. Do you want me to conduct this interview or will you be okay to join me?"

A mournful giggle burst from me, and I wiped my tears away again. "Let me clean myself up and I'll join you. I promise I won't have another outburst."

"All right. If he shows up, I'll wait to start until you arrive." He left me alone in the office to finish pulling myself together. Shame filled me for my outburst, but there was nothing I could do about it now. Again, Merric had handled the situation with grace. Just who was this elf?

I took a few minutes to compose myself before slipping out of the office and heading to my room to check that my makeup didn't make me look weird. First impressions were everything after all. If this was to work, I needed to make good impressions on people. With my abruptness with Liz, I wouldn't have been surprised if she thought I was a fruitcake with a few too many nuts.

When I was ready to face the world again, or maybe just Merric, I left the apartment and headed toward the conference room. The next elf on the list was already inside the conference room with my assistant, and the two were laughing as I let myself in. They both looked at me, and the new elf stood to introduce himself. He was an older elf and his smile warmed me from the inside out.

"Well now, Holly, my you have grown. You probably don't remember me, but I'm Tinsel. The last time I saw you, you and your sister were causing such a stir your parents were ready to rip their hair out." Instead of extending his hand for me to shake, Tinsel wrapped me in a tight bear hug. I didn't remember the elf, but my father had told me stories of him. The two had been close, and still were, but Tinsel had ventured away from Christmas Village to explore the human world.

"Hi, Tinsel. It's good to see you. Papa still talks about you."

"Good. For a while I thought he'd forgotten about me, then I received a message that his youngster was opening up the new bakery, and he wanted me to apply for a position. So, do I qualify?" His belly laugh lightened my spirits and I hugged him again.

"Of course you do, Tinsel. In fact, if Merric agrees with me, I'd like you to be one of the Head Bakers on a floor." I turned to Merric and arched a brow. "Tinself was one of Papa's trainers in the bakery. If anything, he should be running this place."

"Oh, no, young lady. Not a chance. I don't want to lead this shindig. This is all you. Your papa wouldn't have chosen you if he thought I could do better. However, if a Head Baker position is open," he threw his gaze at Merric, "I would gladly accept."

"Then so be it. Who am I to argue with the man who trained Chip?"

"Well, if that's settled, I'm going to find an apartment and move in."

Tinsel left and I took my seat again beside Merric. The hot chocolate was now cooler than lukewarm, but the flavor was still amazing, and I started on the third cup. By the time all of that day's interviews were over, I'd eaten through all of the baked goods Merric had brought me.

Even he'd eaten a muffin during one interview where the lady and her husband had gone on and on until he'd had to cut them off a half an hour and two questions later. Santa only knew where we could put those two where those around them would get their work done instead of talk all day.

Who knew what else the day would bring.

Chapter 9

By the end of the day's interviews, we had a few bakers, mechanics, and janitorial staff. Most ended up where they requested, but a few were moved to other positions where they would have a better fit. Since it was the first day, Merric had made a light schedule so that we ended in the early evening. The rest of the two weeks would have interviews into the late evening. I appreciated the lighter schedule since I was bushed and ready to call it a night by the time we ended.

"Is there anything that you need that I can provide you with?" Merric asked, standing from his chair after our last interviewee had left. He lifted his arms high above his head and stretched.

I shook my head when he stared down at me, which was easy enough with his height, but I was still sitting. "No, I don't think so. There's enough food in my apartment, and I'll be heading to bed early. I'm not looking forward to two weeks of this, though."

"Me either, but we did good today. You did good. You have a way with people that I don't. There were several of them where I had no idea where to put them. They obviously weren't bakers, but you knew what they'd be best at."

Merric pulled me to my feet and led me from the conference room as he spoke. Like always, he walked me to my apartment. I wasn't sure why he did it, but it was nice.

"I'll see you tomorrow morning. Same time?"

He shrugged. "Maybe not so early now that we have a system. Just make sure you're there before the first appointment. Good night, Holly."

"Good night, Merric."

Tonight he stayed until I was inside the apartment. With the door closed behind me, I looked at my apartment. It may not have been fully decorated, but it was still mine and I could do what I wanted with it. I could make it Christmas.

Since my cell phone was still in my office and I didn't want to walk back to retrieve it, I opened the email app to send a message to Merric when I caught sight of a message from Papa with the subject: "You deserve coal for Christmas." That letter could only be from Jolly. Before I opened her message, I sent a quick note to Merric about supplies I wanted. If I didn't send it now, I would forget. Then I opened Jolly's message.

"First, Papa promised to find me a tablet this week. And second, you forgot to mention anything about your new assistant. I'm waiting. Oh, and yes, I chose a new job. However, since you didn't tell me anything about Merric, you have to guess what it is, and I may or may not tell you. We shall see how I feel and how much information you give me. Well, Papa wants this thing back. Love you, sis! Send info soon or I may never tell you my new job."

That crazy nutcase would be the death of me. I was not giving away any information when I was emailing Papa's account. If she thought I would, she was crazy. Lifting my eyes to the city outside, I shook my head at her. However, at some point I'd have to tell her about Merric. Whatever I said, she'd take completely out of context.

I didn't bother replying before turning the tablet's screen off. There would be time, and I needed to think of not only a response for information about Merric, but also what job she could have taken. Even if I told her about Merric, I knew she wouldn't outright tell me what the position was. I either had to guess correctly or find some way to bribe her into telling me.

With the sound up on my tablet, a dinging echoed in my apartment, and I opened the email app to find a message from Merric. "Still haven't found your phone I see. Anyway, I'll have those supplies for you in the morning. Good night." I wanted to argue with him that he didn't have to rush out and provide me what I asked for right away, but already I knew it was useless. Even if I told him that, he'd still come through and I'd have my items in the morning. Silly elf. I sent him a quick thank you and went to make myself dinner.

• • •

Even though Merric had told me I didn't have to show up to the conference room early, I wanted some time to settle in before our first interview. I'd eaten cereal for breakfast again, and in the back of my mind I hoped he'd provide some sweet treats like he had yesterday. I was being spoiled, and I knew I shouldn't become accustomed to it, but it was hard not to when Merric did anything and everything I asked of him.

I was on top of the conference room when I looked up from watching the tiles as I walked, deep in thought. My jaw dropped as my hands covered my open mouth and tears stung my eyes. Unlike yesterday, none fell, but gratitude burned in my heart.

Merric sat at the conference table, ready for the day and watching me, a sly, crooked grin covering his face. I could barely contain the excitement that filled my body as it raced through my blood to every inch of me. Music trickled out of the room, and I recognized it as it played a slow Christmas ballad. Lights and garland were strung around the room. Red bows were attached to every chair, and a long table runner with poinsettia designs laid across the center of the table. A few poinsettias sat on a credenza on my side of the room.

However, those were dull in comparison to the beautiful Christmas tree that stood in the far corner of the room, fully decorated with lights and tinsel. Candy canes hung from branches alongside bright blue and silver ornaments. The star at the top of the tree glittered a bright gold that stole my breath. In fact, the whole room was a Christmas showcase.

"This is amazing," I told Merric when I found my feet and stepped inside. My voice was breathless, and barely more than a whisper as I continued to stare around at the beauty he'd created.

"I can't decorate the whole building for you, but I thought I could start by giving you a small taste of home in your area. I'm no professional decorator, but for now this will have to do."

I shook my head at him as I spun to take it all in. "I can't believe you did this for me."

Merric didn't have a chance to respond as the elevator sounded that it had arrived on our floor. Our first appointment was early. I took my seat beside Merric, who pushed a to-go cup container my way. In my awe of the room, I hadn't noticed the cups and more muffins he'd brought me.

"Thanks," I murmured as a short, spunky elf skipped across the tile hall.

She was about my age with a wide smile. Her eyes lit up when she saw the room, and her reaction matched mine when I saw it, at least I assumed so with the amount of wonder in her gaze. We were forgotten as she entered the room and spun.

While she studied the room, I studied her. She wore fitted jeans with sneakers, but her sweater made her stand out. It was covered in glitter with a decorated tree knitted in the center with pompoms, sequins, and other small decorations sewn onto the fabric. Two sandy blonde buns were pinned in place with red and green bobby pins with jewels at the ends of them. The best part of the ensemble were the large reindeer head earrings she sported in each ear. Since we knew that reindeer didn't pull Santa's sleigh, it was always ironic for an elf to wear anything to do with reindeer.

"Who did this?" she asked, turning to us while pointing around the room. "This is great."

I jerked my thumb in Merric's direction after swallowing a sip of hot chocolate. "He did it."

Her eyes widened at my response. "Wow, really this looks amazing."

"That's what I told him. I'm sorry, but what's your name?"

The elf giggled, finally pulling the chair out across from me and sitting in it. "Sorry, I'm Noel. I'm afraid I become a bit distracted by Christmas decorations. It doesn't matter how many lights I've seen, they always make me smile."

Grinning, I peered over at Merric, hoping he'd understand what I wanted him to know. He nodded and turned his attention back on Noel. "It's nice to meet you and thank you for coming. So, you like Christmas decorations, but do you like decorating?"

"Yes! How could an elf not like to decorate for Christmas? It's in our blood, isn't it?" She was bouncing in her chair with excitement, and I hoped Merric could see that she was the perfect choice to solve my homesickness problem.

"Noel, we have a new position that opened up yesterday," he began, and I wanted to applaud his ability to read me already. "It is a position that will be extremely important, and will likely boost morale. You seem to be the perfect choice for the lead on the decorating team. Will you accept?"

Her eyes grew wide and she covered her mouth with her hands as shock swamped her. "You want me-me- to be the lead decorator?"

That was the perfect title. "You bet," I answered, grinning at the blonde elf. "It has to be someone who finds the beauty in the decorations, but also someone who reacts the way you did to this room. Any elf or human can find this room to be beautiful, but we need someone who is moved by the beauty of the room, someone who feels it, not just sees it. I don't think we'll find a better choice."

"Thank you! Thank you so much!" Noel launched herself out of her chair and raced around the table to wrap her arms around my neck. "This is the greatest opportunity of my life. I can't believe this." She stood back up, hopping up and down in a tiny circle with her hands flailing in excitement.

"We're glad you're excited," Merric laughed. "When the interviews are over, you'll work with me to budget what you need, and you'll go to Holly for ideas of what she wants. The rest is up to you."

"This is a dream come true," Noel cried, tears streaming down her cheeks. "How can I ever thank you?"

"By making this place scream Christmas," I told her. She hugged me again and we bid her farewell.

"Nice choice," Merric commented when the door closed behind Noel. He turned in his chair to stare at me, his eyes narrowed. "Honestly, is this room really that great?"

"It's perfect. I cannot thank you enough for this. It means more to me than you can imagine."

I didn't wait for him to respond, but threw my arms around him and squeezed. It took him a few moments to react and hug me in return. His clothes smelled of evergreen, and for a moment I lost my senses in the scent of home. A moan escaped me as I breathed in again, picturing the Christmas tree yard outside Christmas Village, and memories of choosing the perfect tree played through my thoughts.

"Am I interrupting something?" a gravely female voice asked from the doorway.

I hopped away from Merric, heat rising to my face. A deep blush crept up his neck until he saw our next interviewee. Then he paled beyond what I thought was healthy.

"Aunt Carol. What are you doing here?"

"Why, I'm interviewing for a position, of course. What else would I be here for?"

The older elf stepped up to the table and sat down before I could tell my feet to move. Merric's aunt was applying? Well, of course he had family, so it made sense some of them would join the ranks. However, from the icy glare she shot him and the way he cowered under it, there was some underlying family issue.

"I'm sorry, your name is Carol?" I asked, trying to draw her attention to me so that we could start the interview and I could ask some questions. My curiosity was peeked, and I couldn't wait for her to leave so I could interrogate Merric, if he cooperated.

Her gaze fell on me and she arched an eyebrow. "Your name is Holly?"

"Yes."

"And I take it you're interested in my nephew the way you were hanging off of him when I came in."

I blanched, my mouth popping open and my eyes bulging. Sure, that may have been how it appeared from the outside, but I didn't have those types of feelings for Merric, did I? He was a great friend and assistant, but it wasn't anything more than that. Only, my mouth wouldn't work to tell her that. In fact, my brain forgot what words even were as I stared into those icy eyes.

"Aunt Carol, it wasn't as it appeared," Merric stated, saving me. "She was giving me a hug. That was all."

Yeah, what he said.

"Knowing that you are half your father, I tend to doubt that was some innocent hug."

"Leave my father out of this," Merric growled. I turned my wide-eyed stare on him. I'd yet to hear that tone of voice come out of his mouth,

Carol stared at him for several scrutinizing seconds before nodding and turning her attention back on me. My jaw snapped shut and I faced her with as much courage as I could muster. This woman was a family matriarch, that much was clear, and she was used to getting her way. Well, not in my bakery.

"Well, Holly, what would you like to know?"

"Uh, um, so…" I fumbled for a question before our routine first question popped into my head. "What position are you interested in?"

"A Head Baker. If you want to know my experience, read this." She pulled a folded sheet of paper from her gray wool coat pocket and shoved it across the table to me.

I took a few minutes to read it. Merric didn't bother to appear interested. Out of the corner of my eye I caught him doodling on the corner of a sheet of paper, which was again out of character for him. I had never seen him make any marks on his papers besides to write notes. Tuning him and my curiosity out, I focused on the paper before me.

"Wow, this is quite a work history." I laid the paper down and did my best to stare her straight in the eyes with as much authority as I could muster. "Now, I can tell you have an issue with Merric. I'm not going to be nosy and ask what it is, but what I do want to know is if we give you a Head Baker position, can you take direction from him?"

Her eyes grew a few degrees icier. "I'll have you know that I keep my personal and professional lives separate. When I'm in this building, I'm an employee and will treat him with the same respect I treat you."

Which wasn't much, obviously.

"All right, well that respect starts now. You have the position. We'll be in touch about which floor you'll be over. If there are any problems between the two of you, I will step in. Is that clear?"

"Of course."

I turned my gaze to Merric, who shrugged. "It won't be a problem."

"Good. Well, Carol, that is all. Thank you for coming in."

She didn't bother with a farewell, but stood and strode from the room. I watched her go, wondering how she and the man sitting beside me could be related. As she reached the elevators, I hoped there were no more relatives in the rest of our interview queue.

Chapter 10

"What was that all about?"

Merric groaned, dropping his head onto the table. "Don't ask. Seriously, it's not worth it."

"Your dad?"

"Mom's family doesn't like him. End of explanation."

I wanted to keep pushing, but I could already tell that wouldn't get me anywhere. He'd clam up and we'd be awkward for the next elf coming in. I'd had enough awkward from the last elf to last me a while.

"I'm sorry for the hug, or rather that it appeared the way it did," I muttered when the room remained quiet as we waited.

He lifted his head and smirked at me. "I'm not. I don't receive that many hugs, plus it'll give the family something to gossip about that has some basis for truth. Most of their gossip is conjecture that is so far off I roll my eyes and shake my head way too often when word reaches me."

"Your mom's family sounds awful."

"They're an interesting bunch. Now, here comes our next elf."

THOSE WERE the worst two weeks of my life. Not only were interviews monotonous, Jolly had her personal email now, but she was still refusing to tell me anything since I wouldn't tell her about Merric. She'd broken Vixen, so she knew Merric was young and what he looked like, but she wanted details, and I wasn't forthcoming with any. Our standoff gave my mood a grumpy edge, or maybe it was the continuous rounds of interviews. By the time they were complete, even Merric was downing hot chocolate as fast as I was. When he mentioned buying a machine to make us a cup in the conference room on demand, I fully agreed, and it showed up the next morning, complete with a fresh mug in my place and one in front of him.

I'd finally retrieved my cell phone from my desk and called Papa to check in. There had been nearly thirty messages on the phone, and all were from him wanting to know how I was doing. Since he hadn't been able to reach me, he'd taken to checking up via email. The repairs at Christmas Village were underway, but it would still be after Christmas before they could restart their baking.

"Well, I'll post the list downstairs in the lobby and in the other building so everyone knows where they're supposed to be and at what time," Merric told me as his printer produced the copies be needed. He'd moved down into his newly finished office a few days ago, and though we'd been together in the conference room since then, it appeared lonelier already without his office equipment stuffed in a corner.

"Thanks. I'm hoping tomorrow goes smoothly, but I'm afraid it might not."

"There will be some rough patches," he agreed, "but they'll smooth out. They have to." I caught the words he muttered under his breath and I agreed with his concern. With less than two weeks until the official start date that Papa and Santa had given us, we were cutting it close.

"Merric, when they say we have to have this place rolling by November first, what do they mean exactly?"

"Fully operational: staffed and running at capacity to produce the needed baked goods to meet the demands of the orders. We may not have those last ovens, but we can still produce enough product for the orders we'll receive. Since Chip won't be supplying anything, he's forwarded me his orders. We've picked up a few new clients, larger food chains around the world, but I believe we can handle it all."

"We hope," I added since he would be thinking it.

"We hope."

"Will they fire us if we don't make that deadline?"

He stood from his chair and walked around his desk. The office was much smaller than mine, or at least it appeared smaller since he had by far more office equipment and filing cabinets than I did. "No, but it won't be good. We'll lose accounts and the Christmas spirit we spread with our baked goods will diminish. The end result of losing even one account could be catastrophic down the road."

"And it would all be my fault," I moaned, the stress of the situation rising until it became hard to breathe.

"No, it'll be our fault. I will not let you take the fall alone. After all, everything that took place before you joined me was my doing. If that fails, then the rest follows. And we're not going to fail, remember?"

"Yup. Okay, so you're posting the jobs. What next?"

"I've got some forms that everyone will need to fill out before they can work. Everyone is to show up an hour before their start time to complete them. Then they'll be stored in your office. I have everyone starting in waves tomorrow so that you can go over their job requirements with them. Let's face it, tomorrow will be terrible, but then it should start getting better."

Merric was right, but my nerves were still on edge. "Merric, do you want to take a break when you're done with the paperwork and bake with me?"

He stared at me like I'd grown a third arm. "I thought I wasn't allowed to bake since I didn't know the difference between sugar and sugar?"

Shrugging, I grinned at him and moved to follow him out of his office. A stack of papers sat cradled in his arms, and I hoped he wouldn't accidentally drop them. "I wouldn't trust you to bake on your own, but you are my assistant, so you could assist me."

"Making cookies?"

"I was thinking muffins. Pumpkin spice with some chocolate chips."

"That sounds amazing." He gazed down at the papers in his hands and then back at me, a smirk on his face. "You want to come with me and check out the other building? You haven't been there yet."

"What, you aren't tired of me yet?"

"You're good company." He jerked his head toward the elevators.

I followed him as he led the way. We passed a few elves and I waved and called hello. Merric nodded. Some watched him with odd stares before going back to their business. I assumed their curiosity was about his height since I still couldn't figure out how an elf could be so tall.

A group of elves stepped off the elevator as we reached it, allowing us to walk in without having to wait. Since the elves had free time until starting work tomorrow, they were exploring. Several already knew what their positions were, so they were checking out their space before the rush of tomorrow.

My phone rang as we exited the elevator, and I pulled it from my pocket to see Papa's number across the screen. I motioned for Merric to go ahead and I would join him later, but he shrugged and waited while I answered the phone. However, it wasn't Papa on the other end.

"Holly, you gum drop, you'd better stop evading my questions!" Jolly screeched after I answered.

I'd never been so happy to hear my sister's voice, no matter if she was screaming at me. It was her way of showing she loved me too. In her own odd way.

"It's good to talk to you too, Jolly. How are you? Are you ready to tell me what your new job is?"

"Are you ready to tell me what's going on between you and your new assistant?" I should have known not to bring up the taboo topic.

My expression of panic and horror caused an arched eyebrow from Merric when I glanced at him to see if he'd heard her through the speaker.

"Nothing. Absolutely nothing. Can I call you back?" I asked, my voice cracking.

"He's standing right there, isn't he?"

"Yeah, kinda."

"Kinda? He either is or he isn't."

I stomped my foot against the gray tile. "Is. Now, I need to go, but I'll call you back later."

"I forget how uptight you can be around boys. Sheesh, relax a little, will you?" Jolly feigned annoyance, but I could hear her smiling at my awkwardness. "Okay, okay, I'll stop. I miss you, Holly."

"I miss you too."

"Well, if you're with him, you must be busy, plus I stole Papa's phone and I need to put it back before he notices." Leave it to Jolly.

"I'm glad you borrowed it," I told her, amending her use of the word "stole."

"Me too. Be good. Don't make me come down there. Wait, never mind. Do something to make me come down there. I gotta meet this guy."

"Goodbye, Jolly," I growled, out of patience with that topic.

"Oh calm down. Love you, sis."

"Love you too." I ended the call before she could say anything more about Merric. He gave me a small, worried smile, and I realized I was still staring at him. Fighting a blush, I pushed the phone back in my pocket.

"Everything okay at home?" he asked at the same time the elf that could save me walked through the front door.

"Yeah, it's all good. My sister borrowed Papa's phone to call me and find out how I was. Hey, Noel!" I called across the room, gaining the elf's attention, before redirecting my words back to my assistant. "I actually need to talk to her, Merric. Sorry. Can I have the tour of the other building later?"

"Uh, yes, of course. You're sure you're okay? The look on your face on the phone...you're sure?" Worry oozed from him and I wanted to dig a hole and bury myself in it when I blushed and gave him a stupid smile.

"I'm fine. Jolly can be...pushy, about certain things. She startled me. That's all." Well, the fact that he was questioning me so intently had to mean that he hadn't heard her side of the conversation, right? Until proven otherwise, that was what I chose to believe.

"What's up?" Noel asked me, her eyes jumping between Merric and I. He gave her a slight smile and nod, but refocused on me.

Interlocking our arms, I started dragging Noel toward the stairs. They were less popular than the elevator and I needed to work off some nervous energy that my conversation with Jolly had left behind. Merric's eyes narrowed like he still didn't believe me, but he didn't argue.

"I'll catch you around later," I told him. "We need to talk decorations, and I need some girl time. See you."

"Have fun. Let me know what you come up with so I can make sure it's ordered."

"We will." Turning toward the stairs, I dragged Noel with me until she caught her footing and sprinted up them with me. We were four flights up when I stopped us. This floor was busy with elves investigating the baking stations since most had never seen an elf bakery, but they didn't notice us when I pulled Noel to the wall next to the stairs for privacy. Before I could get a word in, she spoke.

"So, you and Merric, huh?" Noel asked, her eyes twinkling with mischief.

"What? No, it's not like that."

"On what planet? I've seen you two together, and maybe not for long, but I have eyes. That boy is crazy about you, and you have it just as bad." When I only stared at her since words had left me, she scoffed and crossed her arms over her chest and grinned. "You seriously think he decorated your conference room for fun?"

"He did it because I told him I wanted Christmas decorations and I was homesick."

"So he stayed up half the night purchasing decorations and putting them up? Oh, and hauling that tree upstairs? Girl, he likes you, I promise."

"Oh."

Noel threw her head back, her belly laugh echoing up and down the halls. More than one elf stopped what they were doing to stare at us. Now that we had everyone's attention, I did not want this conversation to continue.

Grabbing Noel by the elbow, I dragged the still cackling elf to the nearby staircase and hauled us both up to the next level. Though it wasn't deserted, there were fewer listening ears, and she'd quieted some. Tears streamed down her cheeks and she attempted to wipe them away while I tried to ignore her continued chuckles.

"You know," Noel started, her words choppy with slight gasps between them, "rumor has it that Merric's aunt pretty much caught the two of you making out in the conference room."

My jaw hit the floor. In fact, it may have gone through several floors. I knew elves were gossipers- I mean, I'd grown up in Christmas

Village- but to have a rumor morph that far from the truth was crazy. There was only one place that rumor had started, and me and Carol were about to have a serious elf to elf conversation.

"We were not making out. We weren't even close to that. I was hugging him. That was it. And it wasn't a romantic hug. It was a friendly hug."

She shook her head, rolling her eyes as she did. "Right, and the part where you were smelling him?"

I opened my mouth to argue whatever point she would make, but stopped short. My cheeks flushed and my entire body heated at the memory of his scent. "Uh, yeah, I may have smelled his shirt, but only because it smelled of pine and reminded me of home," I added quickly when Noel opened her mouth. I needed to nip in the bud any other reasons for the smelling that might take on a life of their own in the rumor mill.

"You expect me to believe that?"

"You want to be switched to garbage duty?"

"That's cold."

"Then yes, I expect you to believe that. Okay?"

Noel shook her head and stared around the expansive room. "Well, I still stand by what I said: the man likes you, a lot."

"He's just nice, Noel," I argued.

She held up a hand, stopping me. "Okay, for now let's agree to disagree. Did you actually need to talk to me, or were you trying to escape him. I saw the panic on your face."

"My sister Jolly was teasing me about him and he was standing right there."

"You do like him."

"Noel-."

"I know, I know. I'll leave it alone."

"But yes, I wanted to talk to you. Let's go up to the conference room. And don't say a word. I want to sit is all, and we're talking decorations, so it only makes sense."

"And it's beautiful. I won't argue with the location, but can we take the elevator this time? Running up all those stairs is going to kill me for sure. I'm not out of shape, but I'm not in that great of shape either."

My wicked grin made her tense, and I giggled when she grew wary. "Of course we can take the elevator. I don't want to have to replace you already. Let's go. We have a lot to discuss. After all, we have several floors to decorate before the first of November, and that includes music."

Chapter 11

Noel and I spent most of our time together chatting and getting to know one another. At the same time we did discuss decorating ideas. We also sang our hearts out to the carols playing on the stereo system Merric had procured, and danced around the room until we were out of breath.

Completely breathless, I slumped down into the chair beside where Noel was sprawled out, both of us gasping for breath after singing and dancing to "Grandma Got Run Over By A Reindeer" three times in a row. When I finally caught my breath, I looked out into the hall to make sure we were alone, only to find Merric standing on the other side of the glass with his arms folded and a wicked grin on his face and a mischievous gleam in his eyes.

"How long have you been out there?" I called to him as loud as my hoarse voice could project.

He shrugged, pointed to his ears, and shook his head. Did that mean he couldn't hear me? Well, we did have the music up a bit loud. And he was on the other side of a wall. With the door closed.

"How long has he been standing there?" Noel yelled to me over the music, but I could barely make out her words since her voice was as raspy as mine. So she hadn't heard me call to him, which meant he hadn't heard me after all.

Weak and shaky from the crazy dancing and skipping around the table I'm been a part of, I crawled out of the chair, heading toward the door. Merric stayed where he was in the center of the wall and waited for me to join him on his side of the glass before turning to me, though he didn't come any closer. Noel's cackling rose above the music until the glass door shut behind me. Every word of the music could still be heard on this side, which meant it was way too loud.

"I see you're having fun with your girl time." Merric's grin was pure evil, and I again wished the ground would swallow me.

"How much of that did you see?"

His smile faltered and he scuffed a well shined shoe against the tile. "Enough to know that you're right, music and decorations do make you happy, and you do miss home and your sister."

"I do, but this helps."

"I'm glad." His smile returned and he gazed through the glass at a still singing Noel, though even I could tell she wasn't singing as loud as we had been. "Did you come up with a list of decorations you need?"

"Yes, we did. However, you're going to tell her where to purchase them, and then she'll buy them. You'll wear yourself out trying to keep up with her ideas and plan of attack. I need you focused on other things." His eyebrows rose, an expression that bid me explain what I meant. So I did. "There's only one of me. You know the plan too, even if you don't know everyone's job descriptions by heart or know how to bake. If I'm busy, I need you to be less focused on decorations and more on the day to day running of this place, and let Noel handle decorating. If she needs help, she'll go to you. I already made sure of it."

"So, in short, you need me." His boyish grin was back, and it made me want to flatten his spiky hair for the sake of revenge of his teasing. No one would think our talk innocent if he kept it up, but was it all innocent? I pushed the thought away after momentary contemplation. There was no way he could be interested in me. Why would he be? After all, that first few hours after we met were not my best. Any man would have run from that.

"I need you focused on the job," I corrected, which was followed by a sound of disapproval from Merric.

"Same thing. Now, believe it or not, it's late, and I don't believe you've had dinner. I ordered pizza for you and it'll be delivered shortly. I'll bring it up when it arrives. There's enough for you and Noel to both have plenty, and then some."

"You could join us," I offered, but he shook his head.

"No, but thank you. You girls have fun. For once since you arrived, I'm going to bed early. I'll see you soon with the pizza, and then I'm calling it a night. Don't stay up too late."

"I won't. Thanks."

He waved to Noel and headed for the elevator. After this encounter, I wasn't sure who I would rather have faced more, Jolly or Noel. Since Noel was grinning at me like she knew a secret I didn't and I had nowhere to run, Jolly would have been the safer choice. And that was saying something.

When my alarm blared early in the morning, I wanted nothing more than to throw it across the room, but I couldn't move. Every bone, joint, and muscle in my body ached on a level I'd never known. I'd been sick before, but this took the cake. It took every ounce of energy I had to not only turn the alarm off, but to sit up in bed. Of all the days to be sick, it had to be today.

The pounding in my head grew until I was sure someone was taking a hammer to it when I stood and crossed the room to where my phone sat on the dresser. It took me five minutes to successfully call Merric, and by then I was sitting back on the bed so I wouldn't fall over. He answered on the fourth ring, sounding breathless like he'd made a mad dash to answer it.

"Holly, what's up?"

"I'm sick," I whispered so the pounding wouldn't grow worse.

He paused and a soft sigh came through the phone. "I'm coming over, so when you hear someone knock and come in, it's only me."

The call ended as he hung up, and I struggled to my closet to pull on my robe. It was less for modesty and more to add a layer to my already thick pajamas and comforter. The heat needed to be turned up in the apartment or I would freeze to death, only I didn't know how to adjust the temperature. I'd have to ask Merric to do it when he arrived.

I'd managed to crawl back under the covers when there was a knocking at the apartment door and it opened and shut. Footsteps crossed the living room and came up the hall until Merric stood in the doorway of my bedroom. If I'd been in my right mind instead of wanting to cry from pain and cold, I would have been shocked into falling over that he was wearing jeans and a t-shirt. It had to have been the first clothes he could find to change into or he'd planned to dress comfortable today.

I opened my mouth to greet him, but instead, a sob escaped. Pain lanced through my head and body, but it couldn't stop the tears that leaked from my eyes. Merric was at my side in a second, sitting on the bed beside me and placing a hand to my forehead.

"Wow, Holly, you're burning up, and pardon me, but you look like crap."

I felt worse than I looked. I could guarantee it.

He left my side, racing for the bathroom and returning moments later with a damp cloth that he set across my forehead. I tried to pull away from the painful cold of it, but the bed wouldn't let me move, and Merric refused to remove it when I whimpered. He pulled out his phone, but I was in too much pain and discomfort to hear his words to know who he was talking to.

"Shh, it's okay, Holly. You're going to be okay. Noel is on her way here so I can take care of a few things, and then I'll be back to check on you."

"I'm s-s-sorry," I stuttered through the cold that wouldn't go away.

"This isn't your fault. Relax. We'll take care of you. Do you think you can drink something?"

I wasn't sure, and more tears leaked from my eyes in response. He flipped the cloth over on my forehead, once again torturing me with the cold thing. Then he was gone.

Kitchen cupboards slapped closed, echoing up the hall. The dull sound was amplified from my overactive senses, and I cringed and fought not to cry more at the noise. After the sound of running water, Merric returned holding a small glass half full of water, which he set on my nightstand. He helped me into some sort of sitting position before assisting me to drink. I may not have been strong or steady enough to hold the cup on my own, but I could tilt it a little. When I was done, I turned my face away, and he set the cup back down on the nightstand.

Merric was assisting me to lay back down when my apartment door opened and closed again. I didn't care that someone else was entering my home. My brain was being hacked apart, as was the rest of my body, and I expected my body to turn into a brick of ice any second.

"What can I do?" a feminine voice called from the door before footsteps moved toward my bed.

"Well, human medicines don't really work for elves, so we need to keep her cool. Keep this cloth cold and damp," Merric directed our new companion. I was far too tired to bother opening my eyes to see who it was, and my brain wouldn't try to figure it out either. "Can you stay with her? There's something I need to do."

"Of course I'll stay."

"Thanks. I'll be back soon." Merric leaned over me and cupped my cheek in his hand. "You'll be okay, Holly."

"I'm so cold," I stammered, pushing my face against his warm hand.

"It's the fever. I have to go, but Noel is staying with you. I'll be back soon." His voice was calm, but there was a panicked edge to it that worried me.

"Merric-."

"You'll be okay, Holly. I promise." He removed the cloth from my forehead and placed a kiss to my damp skin. I didn't have the energy or thought process to read more into it than him being a worried friend. He bid me farewell one last time before hurrying from the room. Was he jogging down the hall?

Noel retreated to the bathroom where the sound of more running water met my ears. When she returned, she placed the torturous cloth back on my forehead. It was again freezing cold, and I turned my head to dislodge it. Noel would have none of it.

"Oh, no you don't. Stop that. This is helping you. It's either this or I throw you in the bathtub with it full of cold water. Your choice, miss."

Well, I didn't want the bathtub option, and she would do it. I was certain of that. Instead, I suffered under the damp cloth. At least it heated under the touch of my skin. I was just drifting into some form of sleep when Noel removed the cloth and put a second, freshly chilled cloth in its place. The shock stole my breath and I gasped through it.

Noel was a patient and gentle nurse, though she was blunt when I refused her care. She helped me take sips of water, which cooled my itchy throat. Eventually I stopped arguing about the cold cloth as my headache faded, though the chill remained. Sleep pulled me in and spit me back out. Back and forth I went, only coming to the surface of reality long enough to open my eyes to be sure I wasn't alone, but Noel was always at my side.

I wasn't sure how much time had passed before familiar footsteps entered the hallway, waking me from a light doze. "How is she?"

"Merric?" My voice was as loud as I could muster, but it was still only a whisper.

"Holly, how do you feel?" A cool hand rested against my cheek, but I didn't have the strength to open my eyes. Already sleep wanted to pull me back under into unconscious bliss.

"Terrible."

"Yeah, you don't look or feel any better. That fever doesn't want to go away. Noel, will she drink?"

"Not much. How is she so sick? Elves don't get this sick, at least none that I know of anyway." Noel's words carried her worry even when her actions spoke of calm.

"Sometimes we do, but it's rare. She's been running herself ragged, and I blame myself for most of that. I have an idea. I'll be right back." He placed a kiss to my sweaty temple before leaving the room. Noises in the kitchen perked my interest enough to fight sleep. I already had water. What else could he possibly want in there?

Prodding woke me from a sleep I hadn't realized I'd fallen into, and a hand cupped the back of my head and neck. Merric lifted me so that I was sitting up enough so I wouldn't choke on the liquid in the mug he pressed to my lips. "Drink this."

A sugary scent swam around me, awaking my senses. "Mmm," I moaned, recognizing the smell of the best drink on Earth. Hot chocolate filled my mouth, and I swallowed greedily until the mug was empty. It wasn't too rich, which meant he'd used water instead of milk, but it was still divine compared to straight water.

"That's my girl," Merric murmured as I drank, and my heart skipped a beat. Did male friends say such things? I didn't dwell on that thought long enough to solve it, but licked my lips to make sure I didn't miss any of the prized liquid.

"Will you look at that," Noel laughed. I opened my eyes and found her standing behind Merric, who sat with me on the bed, peeking over his shoulder. "I guess all it takes is a little bribery to drink, huh?"

"More like she's an elf," Merric laughed. "Hot chocolate can be the best medicine for our kind. Now relax, Holly. Go back to sleep."

"I'm so cold," I whimpered as he laid me back down. The hot chocolate had helped warm me, but my extremities were still frigid.

The bed groaned and shifted as Merric moved, and I was pleasantly surprised when he laid beside me on top of the covers and his arms wrapped around my body. When Noel cuddled me on my other side, I didn't know what was happening. At least she didn't try to mimic Merric's cuddling style. She could tease me all she wanted to later, but the contented moan I emitted had less to do with the heat they provided, and more to do with the man who lay beside me. When this was over, how was I supposed to react to him? Could I act normal? Or would I blush every time he looked at me? Those questions would have to wait for another day because sleep settled over me as I pushed closer to the man who held me.

Chapter 12

The fever finally broke and I slept uninterrupted for as long as I could. Occasionally I would wake long enough to drink, but then I fell back into a dreamless sleep. When I woke feeling rested, more hot chocolate and a plate of fresh chocolate chip cookies waited for me. Everything else in the room was forgotten except the plate of yummy goodness.

Straining against my covers, I finally gave up reaching the cookies when my tired muscles gave out and I collapsed back onto my pillow. A deep, humored chuckle came from across the room. I peeked an eye open to find Merric standing in the bedroom doorway. Otherwise, the room was empty.

"How do you feel?" He crossed his arms and leaned against the door frame, his boyish smile lighting his face. While deep crows feet and dark purple circles around his eyes marked his lack of sleep, the relief in his eyes burned bright.

"You're wearing jeans," I laughed to which he shook his head with a soft chuckle.

"You're delirious. Want a cookie?"

"Yes!"

Merric pushed himself away from the doorframe and came to me. With little effort, he lifted me so that I could sit and placed the plate of cookies in my lap. Before taking a seat in the chair beside the bed, he snagged a cookie and was out of reach before I could grab it back.

"Silly man," I muttered. Grinning, with a slight blush heating my cheeks, I nibbled on my first cookie until I realized that Merric's smile had faltered and he appeared deep in thought and…awkward?

"We need to talk," he announced, and I set my cookie back on the plate.

Had I said something in my sleep that I shouldn't have? Or done something? Or was this something about the way he felt?

Whatever horrified expression was on my face made Merric grin when he looked up at me. "Relax, Holly. I don't know what you think I'm going to say, but it can't be as bad as your face says it is. First, I called Chip and told him you were sick. I thought he should know, so when you're feeling up to it, you need to call Candy. She's worried about you. It was all Chip could do to keep her at the North Pole. If you had become worse, I would have sent for her, but me and Noel had it all under control."

"Thanks."

"You're welcome. Now, the second bit of news, and I hope you won't be angry with me or want to take my head off, but I postponed the start date for most of the elves. Let me explain," he told me quickly, holding up a hand to stop my comment. "I started those who would be taking inventory so they could begin to become used to the task and find everything. The janitors and downstairs office staff also started. Most of those that haven't begun to work are the bakers, but I don't know anything about baking or how this will work. That's all you."

"How long have I been sick?" I tried to be rational and not be upset with him because what he said was true, but I was losing the battle. "How long, Merric?"

"Three days, but we still have time. It's not like we've been idle. Well, I have, but the bakery elves haven't. Tinsel helped divide them into teams based on what they will be baking. Aunt Carol assisted him. They want a meeting with you and the other Head Bakers when you're up to it. They said they can take it from there."

"How long do we have until our deadline?" My brain was still too tired to do the calculating. Three days was too long if we had to have orders ready to ship, or already shipped, by the first. When Merric squirmed, a pit opened in my stomach. "What else, Merric?"

"There's a week and a half until our deadline."

"But?"

"Right before you called me to say you were sick, I received an email from Santa saying that he, Mrs. Claus, and Chip will be here on the first to inspect our work and help us celebrate."

Even the few nibbles of cookie in my stomach turned to lead and my weakened body grew heavy. Cool hands cupped my face and forced me to look up into pale ocean eyes. How had I not noticed that beautiful color before now?

"We have time. All of the elves are aware of our deadline and want to meet it as much as we do. But," he slapped his thighs and stood up, "the only concern you should have tonight is resting and eating those cookies. Do you want something with a little more substance?"

"Pizza."

Merric's smile widened. "I've created a monster."

I had to agree. However, I did disagree with him on another point. "Merric, I need to meet with the Head Bakers tonight." He tried to argue but I stopped him. "We need to start baking tomorrow. With only a week and a half left to work out the kinks, we have to start first thing in the morning."

Merric leaned in close so that our noses were mere inches apart, and I had to fight to focus on his face. "Holly, even if I agreed with having a meeting tonight, none of them would show up for it, so I'm not going to waste my time and theirs by telling them you want one. They know how sick you've been and that you need rest."

"Please. I won't sleep if we don't have this meeting."

"Not a chance." When I only gave him an irritated glare, which included furrowing my brow, he chuckled and grinned at me. "If I have to tell them we're having a meeting, and I remind you they won't come, then I'm not ordering you pizza. It's your choice."

"Sometimes I don't like you." With a groan, I attempted to untangle the covers, but like before, I could not figure it out, nor did I have the strength. Had I tied a knot in my sleep with these things? I was ready to scream when Merric's hands pushed mine away and he easily untangled my legs and lifted the covers off of me. I attempted to stand, but he stopped me with a hand on my shoulder.

"Now, where are you planning to go?"

"To the bathroom."

In one swift movement, he lifted me from the bed to cradle my body against his chest. After sweating for three days straight there was no doubt that I stunk, but he didn't comment or complain, but carried me to the bathroom. The scent of evergreen clung to him and this time I basked in it without embarrassing both of us by sniffing him. When we arrived at our destination, he set my feet on the floor and closed the door, yelling through it he was ordering pizza. It wasn't the best meal to eat after being sick, but elves weren't meant to eat much health food, at least what humans considered healthy.

By the time I finished my business and had washed my face and brushed my teeth, I was beginning to feel normal again, if not a bit exhausted in the process. Merric wasn't in my room when I emerged from the bathroom, and I couldn't hear him in the apartment. If he was concerned about me falling on the way to the bathroom, he needed to remember I had to come back, unless he thought I would take a while. I should have showered, but I didn't have the strength. Tomorrow would be one long day.

Grabbing my phone on the way back to bed, I crawled under the sheets and dialed Papa's phone. I was expecting to hear his mellow voice, not the whirlwind explosion that was Jolly on the other end, screaming into the phone.

"Please tell me this is Holly, and please tell me you're all right!"

I whipped the phone away from my ear, sure I was now completely deaf. Her overdramatic displays needed to be quieter. "Yes, it's me, and yes, I'm better."

"You sure?"

"Yes, I'm positive that I'm feeling better. Still tired and weak, but I'm awake. Now, is Mama there? And don't you eavesdrop because this is personal and beyond boring."

Jolly huffed, and though I couldn't see her, I knew she'd rolled her eyes. "You do realize this is me you're talking to, right? When have either of us said or done anything boring?"

"Two weeks of interviews will have you eating your words," I grumbled, staring up at the ceiling. "If you're ever given the opportunity to participate in such an occasion, say no. Your brain will thank you for it."

"Wow, I guess you could talk about something boring after all. However, if you were talking interviews, you'd want Papa. Since you want Mama, I can only assume...boy?" She giggled and I pictured myself slapping her upside the head over and over, like it played on a loop.

"Jolly, please, I'm tired. Exhausted really, and when my pizza arrives, all I want is to eat and go to bed, and if I don't talk to Mama now, I'll have to wait and talk to her after pizza. Please." It was never a good idea to beg Jolly. Usually it meant further harassment, but my dear sister took pity on me, for the first time in her life. Undoubtedly it would be the last.

"Holly, how are you? Merric called and said you were pretty sick. He has a level head, so when he sounds worried, you have to know it's bad." Mama's words blurred together, and my tired mind had to fight to keep up with what she was saying.

"Mama, slow down, please. Still waking up here. And I'm fine."

She chuckled, her nerves relaxing when she heard my voice. "Oh, Holly, are you sure you're all right? I've been so worried."

Now it was my turn to roll my eyes. "Yes, I know you've all been worried. I figured that out when Jolly decided to break my eardrum."

"Sorry about that. She reached the phone first."

"Yeah, don't let her do it again or I'm never calling home again." It was a fib, but I hoped it stressed my point. When Mama continued to laugh, I knew I'd missed the point with her.

"What is it you wanted to talk about, dear?"

Hesitating, I spoke softly into the phone, and because I wasn't certain I really was alone in the apartment. What if Merric was laying down on a couch in the living room? I would hate for him to overhear this conversation, especially since it was about him.

"Boys. Well, a boy."

"Oh dear. I was wondering if we'd be having this conversation soon."

"Mama?" My heart skipped a beat when I heard Jolly squeal. "Can you go somewhere private? Please? She can interrogate me later, but I want this to be private for now."

"Of course." There was shuffling and plenty of whining and threats from Jolly, but soon they dimmed and a door clicking shut reached me through the phone. "There, you're safe. I'm trapped in my bedroom and Papa has wrangled her to help him bake cookies. Since the bakery is closed for the season, any elves who can bake are being asked to make cookies at home for now. We're trying to ration and save some for Christmas time, or until you start baking enough to send us."

My groan came without warning, and I couldn't hold it in, even if I wanted to. "To be honest, I don't know if we're going to make the deadline, Mama. I'm trying to stay positive, and I'm hoping for a Christmas miracle, but that's unlikely."

"Why?" she asked, her voice echoing her curiosity.

"Because, who's ever heard of a Christmas miracle at the beginning of November? It's still practically Halloween, and there is no way that a Christmas miracle is happening then." I knew enough about the holiday that I was certain there was nothing good coming from it. After all, ghosts, goblins, zombies, and other ugly, disgusting creatures didn't scream "Christmas miracle" one bit. They were "death by heart attack" worthy.

"Okay, yes, you may not have a Christmas miracle in October or November, though I would argue that you could. However, there are plain miracles, and those happen no matter what time of year it is. I believe that if you try your hardest and don't give up hope and faith, you'll have your miracle. Plus, you still have time, and I know you, Holly. You don't give up when a job is half done. If you put your mind to it, there's nothing you can't do."

A week ago I had her hope and belief that we could do this, but with a week and a half left and not one cookie baked, I wasn't sure we'd make it after all. It would take every ounce of dedication these elves had, and I didn't know any of them well enough to know if they'd pull us through this or if they'd give up faith before we met our deadline.

"Don't give up hope, Holly. You've come so far already."

Shaking my head, I closed my eyes and breathed a soft sigh. "I miss home. I miss the lights, the singing, the snowball fights, the colors, the snow, everything. It's so plain here and boring. Merric was kind enough to decorate the conference room for me, but when I'm not there, I don't know where I am."

"Merric updated Papa and told him you had an elf decorating the building. How is that going?"

"I don't know. I've been sick and asleep for days, remember?"

Mama's bubbly laugh made me smile, even though I wanted to have nothing to do with being happy. When she was happy, you couldn't help but smile along with her. It was just who she was.

"Yes, I remember. Now stop being so pessimistic. It isn't like you. Get some rest and you'll feel better, and drink more hot chocolate. That will help you, and play some Christmas music. Ask Merric for decorations for your apartment. I'm sure he'll be willing. And when the bakery starts up, you get in there and get your hands dirty with dough. That will help you feel even better."

I could already smell the scent of the dough. "Sugar cookies. I'm going to start with sugar cookies. And then I'll move to butter cookies."

"Yes, I approve of those choices. And don't forget muffins and breads. Nothing beats a good fruit cake."

"Thanks, Mama. I knew I'd feel better after talking to you. Maybe this will work after all. And you're right, I'll need to ask Merric for more decorations." I already had, and he'd surprised me with decorating the conference room. He must have forgotten about the decorations I'd asked for while he was doing that. Having a decorated apartment would do wonders for my mood. A Christmas tree set against the New York City backdrop would brighten my mood, and watching the lights flicker as I sat in the dark room with my mug of hot chocolate would almost be like sitting at home.

"Speaking of Merric," Mama laughed, and I blushed. "You wanted to talk to me about a boy?"

Chapter 13

I threw a pillow over my head, wishing now that I'd never said anything at all on the subject, but I'd already started this mess. I might as well finish it. Or talk it over with Mama and never bring it up again. It appeared I would be avoiding all calls with Jolly for the next month. Maybe two.

"Yes, I wanted to talk to you about a boy."

She waited, but when I didn't give any further information, she pressed me. "Would that boy be Merric?"

"Yes. How do you know him, anyway? It sounds like you do when you talk about him." Maybe she knew something that would help me understand why Papa had chosen him above every other elf. After all, wouldn't Papa have chosen an elf who could bake as my assistant?

"I don't know him well. Mostly I know of him. His mother and I were friends growing up. We've stayed in contact over the years, and we've told each other about our children. When Papa was looking for an elf who could assist with the human aspects of the bakery, I thought of Merric. He went to human school and studied business, so he's well equipped to handle the position."

Merric went to human school? I'd never heard of an elf doing that before. What had possessed him to do that? Maybe living more in the human world intrigued him into trying it, and he obviously liked to learn if he finished.

"Mama...I think I like him." The words were soft as a whisper, and as I spoke them, the truth sunk into my heart that I more than liked him. I was falling head over heels for that boyish grin, and his companionship. "When I'm with him, I feel whole. It's a lot like how I feel when I'm with Jolly, but it's different and hard to explain. He's so sweet, and I think he may like me too, but I'm not sure. Well, Noel says he likes me, and I'm scared that I'm reading more into everything he's done since because I'm looking for it. What if he doesn't like me like that? What if I'm making it all up in my head?" That would be humiliating beyond words.

"Oh, Holly, it's okay. And it's normal to have those feelings. This is your first real crush. Can I tell you something about male elves?"

"Uh huh." Anything that could help me sort out this situation would be better than being lost and floundering in it.

"Males fall faster and harder than us females. If he's showing his interest then he likes you, a lot. What makes you think he may like you?"

My mind drew a momentary blank, and nothing came to mind besides his grinning face. "Um, well he did decorate the conference room for me like I said earlier. I told him I was homesick, and he must have stayed up half the night to find decorations and put them up. Oh, and he also bought a real tree to put in there too. And…and when I was sick he called me his girl, like 'That's my girl' and kissed my forehead. Am I losing my mind, Mama?"

"Oh, sweetheart, no you are not losing your mind. Your friend Noel thinks he likes you?"

"Yeah. She mentioned it to me, but I couldn't see it. Maybe now I can? Or maybe I was just denying it. Since I spent most of my time in Christmas Village with Jolly and Vixen, I'm not sure how boys work."

Mom laughed long and hard, and I was sure she was crying by the time she stopped. "Oh, I doubt if you'd spent any time with boys here you would understand them any better than you do now. They don't understand us, and we don't understand them. I've been married to your papa for over twenty years now and sometimes I still don't understand what he's thinking."

She'd made comments like that while I grew up, but now I understood to some degree what she meant. Now I was the one wishing that men came with owner's manuals. I was looking for one that said, "If you want to know if he likes you, press here." Then again, maybe I wouldn't want to know if he said, "No."

"Where is he now?" Mama asked when I remained silent, deep in thought.

"Ordering me pizza. Or I think that's what he's doing. He carried me to the bathroom and left, and I haven't heard from him since. For all I know he's in the living room and can hear me talk." A shiver ripped through my body and I hoped again that wasn't the case.

"No, that doesn't sound like him. If he could hear such a personal conversation, I doubt he'd eavesdrop. His mama would have raised him better than that." I didn't have to see Mama to know she was shaking her head as she spoke. Crossing my fingers, I prayed she was right. When I was on my way back to bed, I should have at least shut my bedroom door.

A light knock sounded on the apartment's front door seconds before it clicked shut behind someone. The scent of pizza drifted down the hall as footsteps followed. Relief swamped me, and I sighed into the phone.

"Mama, Merric and the pizza just arrived. I have to go so I can eat or I may end up biting off one of his arms."

"Hey now," he teased, poking a finger into my side through the blanket. "I heard that."

She giggled, and heat burst through me, starting at the place his finger had touched and it worked its way all the way to my face. "You may be right, Holly. Well, I'll let you start eating. Wouldn't want the boy to lose any body parts to your famished senses."

"I love you, Mama."

"I love you too. Keep feeling better."

"I will. Goodbye."

Merric lifted the pillow from my head as I hung up the phone. He held a slice of pizza in his hand and it hung above me in the air, like a carrot being waved in front of a starving rabbit. If he wasn't careful, maybe he would lose an arm tonight.

"Are you hungry, elf?" He waved the pizza in front of my face while I sat up and snatched for it, completely missing it as he pulled away. I tried again, but was way too slow. When I missed a third time, I glowered at him and stuck my tongue out.

Merric sat on the edge of the bed and held the slice in front of my mouth with the tip of the pizza nearly touching my lips. I stared at it, then up at him, and back at the pizza. Was I supposed to take it or bite it? And if I bit it...was that flirty? My eyes flew back to him, begging him to tell me what to do. With a grin, he pushed the pizza against my lips.

"Open up and take a bite. I want to know what you think. It's a different flavor than those I ordered before. In fact, it's a new flavor my friend is trying and he wants opinions."

Opening my mouth, I leaned in to take a bite of the pizza, never taking my eyes off of Merric. He sported a crooked grin when he lowered the slice while I chewed. The tastes in my mouth distracted me from his searching gaze, and before he could stop me, I stole the pizza from his hands.

"That good?" he asked when I took another bite without telling him what I thought of the taste. Instead, I nodded as I chewed, famished. The few cookies and hot chocolate I'd eaten hadn't filled me like the pizza would. "Good, I'm glad you like it. I'll be sure to tell him it's a hit."

Merric stood and swiped a slice from the box and sat back down on the bed, even though the chair was still vacant. Truth be told, I didn't want him to take the chair any more than he appeared to want to sit in it.

"Thank you for the pizza, and for taking care of me. I appreciate it more than you know." And it wasn't just while I was sick that he was taking care of me. He'd been doing it since I'd arrived.

After swallowing his bite of pizza, Merric smiled. "It's been my pleasure." Then his smile faded and he studied the pizza in his hand while he spoke. "Honestly, when I heard your voice over the phone when you told me you were sick, I knew something was wrong, and I couldn't reach you fast enough. You're always so bright and peppy that to see you in tears, I knew you were miserable. And that fever... please do not scare me like that again."

"I'll try not to, but it wasn't exactly my fault in the first place."

"True, but you can start off on the right foot by finishing that pizza and going back to sleep. I know there's no sense in telling you to take the morning off and move slow, but I wish you would."

Since my mouth was full of pizza, I shook my head until I was able to swallow and talk without a mouth full of food. "Absolutely not. We can't afford to lose any more time. Though, I promise that if I become weak I'll take a break. Once I have the bakers all set, there shouldn't be much for me to do besides check in with them and make sure everything is running smoothly."

"But you don't think it will be smooth. I can see it on your face," he remarked when I arched an eyebrow at him. "You're still worried about something, and I think it's that even after we start baking, something will go wrong."

"Cookies burn, bread is doughy, cakes sink...you name it, it can happen. These aren't professional bakers we have here."

"They just need a little help and expert advice. Plus, they'll have a Head Baker on each level. Don't be so worried. Have a little faith." Merric handed me another slice of pizza when I finished the first. "Now eat. I'll take the rest and put it away. You can have it for breakfast."

My eyebrows shot up. Did he say I could have pizza for breakfast? The thought had never occurred to me, but it was suddenly the best option available. Mixed with hot chocolate of course.

"Good night, Holly. Call me if you need me again." He waved goodbye, and I called a farewell after swallowing.

With him gone, the room was empty. Maybe it was because he'd rarely left me alone since I'd come here and I'd never really been alone back home either. While that was plausible, I knew it wasn't the reason. I liked him, and it was him I missed, not his company. The apartment door clicked shut and the joy he'd brought with him sank to a pit in my stomach. Finishing up the pizza, I threw the covers over my head and hoped that more sleep would improve my mood. It couldn't possibly hurt it any. As Mama had said, I was far too pessimistic and sleep would help.

Sunlight slipped under the curtains in my bedroom when I woke up, curling my body into a tight ball as I relaxed deeper into my plush pillow. That was until I realized that if the sun was up, I was late. My alarm hadn't gone off. Had Merric turned it off while I was sick and purposefully not turned it back on?

Slipping from bed, I couldn't stop smiling. My optimistic mood was back and I was feeling more like my old self. Today would be a long, hard day, but if we could pull this off, it would be worth it. After a quick shower, I changed and finished my morning routine, complete with cold pizza, and left my apartment with a skip to my step.

Voices echoed up the hall, and as I turned the corner near my office, I found their origin. The Head Bakers sat with Merric in the conference room, and each held a cup of hot cocoa. Merric did a double take when he saw me approach, and his already smiling face lit with excitement at seeing me. I focused on his aunt on the other side of the room to stop myself from blushing, but in the end, it didn't help. Heat still rose to my face and I was sure it was as bright as the poinsettia sitting in the center of the table.

Noel saved me by rushing to give me a giant hug. "You had me so worried!"

"I'm sorry. I didn't mean to get sick. What are you doing here?" I asked, hugging her back as tightly as she held me.

"I wanted to be sure you were all better. Merric said you were, but I had to see you for myself, and someone needed to add some Christmas cheer to this group," she explained stepping back and nodding to the Head Bakers. "You'd think they'd all forgotten what Christmas feels like."

"Excuse me?" Carol asked Noel, arching an aggressive eyebrow at my bubbly friend.

"You heard me. How are we supposed to make Christmas cookies when none of you were the least bit excited for Christmas before I stepped in here? After all, we're the ones who are putting Christmas in the cookies!"

The older woman rolled her eyes, but stayed silent. It was my turn to take over this meeting. I was pumped and ready to smell cookies and cakes baking.

"Okay, let's do this," I told them, sitting in the chair closest to me, which placed me between Tinsel and a soft spoken woman named Frost. Both smiled at me, and Frost hid a giggle by sipping from her mug as I bounced with excitement in my chair. "Okay, you all know what floor you're on and who you've got working with you, correct?"

Heads nodded, and Merric slid a sheet of paper across the table to me. An identical sheet sat on the table in front of him. I studied it for a moment before recognizing it as the list we'd made of the items we would bake.

"You all have a specialty," Merric began, gaining everyone's attention. "You'll each be assigned a specific type of cookie, bread, or cake to bake. Some of you may receive two, which means you'll rotate between them depending on the demand for each."

"If the demand for both types is high, you'll separate your floor in half. Half will bake one item while the other half bakes another type," I cut in. More heads nodded, but everyone remained quiet as they listened.

Merric set his pen to the paper. "I'll read the list off. When I'm finished, if you have a preference, I'll write your name by it. There will be no arguing. If two of you want the same, Holly will choose which of you receives the opportunity. You will not treat her with disrespect if she doesn't choose you or you will not be a Head Baker. Understand?"

When no one objected to the idea, I laughed. "Let's hurry up. Time's wasting."

Chapter 14

Noel hadn't found a way to blast Christmas music throughout the whole building yet, so she'd improvised and bought several sets of speakers and devices that could hold thousands of songs and loaded each up with music. There was one per floor and as I walked off the elevator onto the second floor, the music greeted me. My smile was so big it almost hurt my face.

It wasn't just the sound of music that had me smiling, but the new decorations as well. Icicle lights twinkled along the walls and garland draped across the ceiling from one end of the building to the other. Candy canes of varying flavors sat in Mason Jars at each work station. To top it off, a brightly lit star hung from the ceiling in the center of the room casting a warm glow over the area nearest it.

"This is beautiful," I breathed, stunned that Noel could get this much decorating done in three days, even with a small team of elves helping her.

"I hoped you'd like it," she laughed, placing her hands on her hips as she inspected her work right along with me. "We started with the first floor, and are only up to the fifth floor, so we still have some work to do, but it's coming along nicely."

"I'll say it is."

"Speaking of coming along…how are things coming with a certain male elf?"

She grunted when I shoved her off balance. Now was not the time to discuss that, especially with him talking with Silver, the floor's Head Baker, on the other side of the room. Music or not, I didn't want our conversation to carry over to him, or anyone else for that matter.

"We'll talk about it later. Girls night. My room. Tonight."

Noel grinned before excusing herself to go work with her team. When she left, I crossed the room to join Merric and Silver. The middle-aged man was a few inches taller than me, and like everyone else, was dwarfed by Merric. As they spoke, elves drifted up the stairs, or ventured off the elevator onto our floor. When most of the elves had gathered toward the center of the room, or continued to the higher floors, Silver sighed.

"Well, I suppose I'd better start becoming acquainted with this bunch and have them set up their stations. I hope some of them know how to bake." He shook Merric's hand and turned to me. "Do you want to say anything to them first?"

I hadn't thought about it, so I shrugged. "Sure, why not."

We crossed the room, and without saying a word, gained the elves' attention. One by one they tapped one another on the shoulder and pointed toward me until silence hung over us. Well, as silent as a room blaring Christmas music can be.

Clearing my throat, I stepped closer to them. "Hello, everyone. Thank you for being on time to your job today. This is your floor, and Silver will tell you what it is you'll be baking when I'm finished. Before you start, I want to make sure you all remember why it is we're baking these cookies. We're helping to spread Christmas love and cheer. Without us doing this, the world would be a darker, colder place. It's our one time of year when we can send the Christmas spirit out in abundance. Now, let's get to work. We've got a lot of orders to catch up on."

Cheers rang out, echoing off the walls and drowning out the music, and it took Silver several attempts to quiet the elves. At least some of them could feel the Christmas spirit, even if some of the elves were a bit grumpy. When they drew silent once again, I stepped back and Silver took my place.

"Our job will be making Chocolate Chip Cookies," he announced, and was met by some squeals, which were quickly hushed so Silver could continue. "Today we'll be setting up our stations. Each station has a recipe. If you've rarely baked, try to partner with someone who is an avid baker. If you have questions, please do not hesitate to ask me or Holly, if she's available. All those wishing to bake today after their station is set up may do so, though it is not required. Now, find your partner, split off, and happy baking."

Chatter filled the room as elves found partners and claimed their baking stations and became familiar with them. Merric looked so out of place as he scanned the room that I giggled. He caught me staring and laughing, and shrugged before shaking his head.

"I'm out of my league down here. Since I'll only be in the way, you can find me in my office if you need me. There's a few emails I have yet to respond to, and I need to organize our orders so we know exactly what we need. It'll be synced to the app on your tablet when I'm done. You can let the Head Bakers know when you receive it."

I grimaced, thinking of all the orders we needed to fill already. Some customers began their holiday preparations early. "Don't make it too overwhelming and I won't panic."

"I'll start with the three with closest deadlines. You behave, and take a break when you need it. We can't afford for you to be sick again because you overexerted yourself."

After assuring him I'd take it easy, though we both knew I would be hard pressed to do that, Merric waved farewell and disappeared up the stairs. With elves still using the elevators, it was fastest to walk, though I wasn't sure he'd be able to move tomorrow if he walked all the way up to his office.

I spent the next half an hour walking with Silver around his floor, talking to his bakers. Some had simple questions about baking, which set loose a troupe of toy soldiers in my stomach, but overall, most understood what they were to do. A few venturesome teams asked Silver for some ingredients to test out a batch or two. Knowing that if I stayed on this floor once they started baking I'd never leave, I bid Silver farewell and walked up to the next floor. If I wanted to stop by every floor today, I needed to pick up my pace.

It soon became apparent that I'd never make it to every floor. Carol was my next stop, and her floor had my stomach growling with the scent of cinnamon and molasses. The cold pizza for breakfast had already been digested, and my stomach growled noisily to tell everyone I'd skipped lunch. With perfect timing, Noel appeared with a mug of hot chocolate and a plastic wrapped sandwich.

"Merric asked me to bring you this. Seems he knew you wouldn't stop to eat." She handed the sandwich over before setting the mug on the closest table. "How's the tour going?"

"Slow, but good." I stuffed the first bite of the sandwich in my mouth and moaned as the assortment of flavors danced on my tongue. That man knew good food when he tasted it, and I was more than happy that he shared that knowledge with me. My waistline may not like it, but my taste buds sure did, and who could argue with those?

"Let me guess, this floor is gingerbread cookies. Yup, I'm going to need to stay away from this floor." Noel stared around the room as the elves chose cookie cutters for their work to begin tomorrow. Unlike the floor below, no one here was attempting a batch of cookies today. Noel groaned and her shoulders slumped. "Who am I kidding? I'm going to have to avoid every floor of this place."

After taking a swig from my mug, I agreed with her. There was nothing as tempting as baked goods right out of the oven. That thought had me making a mental note to stop by each floor first thing in the morning to remind the Head Bakers to announce that no one was to gorge themselves on the sweets or we'd never have enough.

As if he'd heard me, my tablet dinged, letting me know I'd received an email, and sure enough, it was from Merric letting me know the first cookie order was available in the cookie app on my tablet. When I opened the app and took a look, I wanted to puke. It was one of the largest companies we served, and their first order was always their smallest. The orders only grew in size as the season progressed.

"Are you all right? You look sick again." Noel placed her hand on my forehead, but I shook it off.

"I'm fine. Merric sent me some information." Without further explanation, I checked the order due date. One week. We were doomed.

Instead of dwelling on the order and its subsequent deadline, I made my way up to the next floor. And the next. By the time I finished with the cookie floors, my body was complaining I'd overworked it. Sore and tired muscles yelled at me as I climbed up to the first muffin level. Tinsel took one look at me before shooing me upstairs.

Though I knew it was best if I went straight to my office to relax, I ended up stepping off the elevator on Merric's quiet floor. Since I'd yet to use my office for any work whatsoever, I couldn't help wonder why

I even had one. Maybe one day I would find out. For now I was too busy panicking and making sure every floor was under control.

Merric glanced up with wide eyes when I knocked on his open door. "Holly, sit, please." He motioned to a less than comfortable looking chair across from his desk, but my legs were too tired to argue. A soft sigh escaped me when I sat and found the chair wasn't as uncomfortable as it appeared. "How's the baking progress coming? Sorry I bailed on you. I figured you had it under control and I'd be in the way."

My grin matched his. "Everything is going well. Some floors have begun to bake, probably trial runs before the official baking begins tomorrow. The elves who are in charge of boxing up the goods and setting them aside are all set and ready to go, and the inventory elves are prepared to restock the Head Bakers' supplies as needed. You might be receiving an inventory order form soon. If I ever figure out how to do it."

From what Merric and Papa had both explained to me, the inventory elves would each use a paper form to record the numbers. They'd give those papers to the head of that department, who would give them to me. I'd enter that information into the app on my tablet and work from there to submit an order to Merric. It sounded like a lot of work, and Papa agreed, but he also mentioned it would keep me in the loop of what was being used to notice if we had a problem.

"When you need to order the first time, let me know and we'll walk through it together. Would that be okay?"

I nodded to him, a yawn punctuating my answer. "I was supposed to have a girl's night with Noel tonight, but I'm considering bailing on her. Either that or I'll fall asleep during the middle of the movie."

"She won't mind. She knows you need your sleep after being sick. You've done well today. To celebrate, would you like to go out for dinner? My treat of course."

My heart stopped and I stared at him.

"What?" His grin fell to a frown and worry creased his brows. "If you don't want to go, you don't have to. Sorry, you said you were tired. I shouldn't have suggested going out."

Shaking myself from my shocked state, I stopped him. "No, it's fine. Dinner sounds delicious. You have great taste in food, so I'm sure it'll taste wonderful and be relaxing. I just need to know...is this personal or work related?" As soon as the words left my mouth, even though I'd debated saying them, I wanted to kick myself. Hard. Over and over. Afterward I'd put my foot in my mouth and swallow. Jolly would likely hang her head in shame and never speak to me again if she knew I'd asked such a thing. "Never mind. Forget I asked."

The toy soldiers in my stomach were back and marching at full speed. To keep myself from watching Merric's reaction to my inappropriate question, I focused on my hands. The nails needed a coat of bright red polish, or at least that's what Jolly would tell me. Vixen would shake her head at us.

Large hands reached down to take mine, and I looked up to find Merric's face inches from mine. My lungs forgot how to work, and I was sure that I was about to suffocate. While he kept my hands in one of his, he lifted the other to brush his fingertips along my cheekbone. His ocean eyes were depthless as they bored into me.

"Holly, I'd like you to come to dinner with me, and yes, it's personal. I'm not sure what elves in the North Pole would call it, but down here, we call it a date."

"Yeah, that's what we call it too." My voice was so airy it was almost a whisper. Merric was asking me out on a date? My first date? And here I was staring at him like a crazy woman. I needed to snap out of whatever funk shock was throwing me in. "Yeah, I'd love to go on a date with you."

His wide, boyish grin grew into a full smile, and he lifted my hands to his lips one by one to leave a kiss on the back of them. "Thank you. Now, what are you in the mood for?"

A shy blush heated my cheeks and I ducked my head again. "Whatever food you want. You know the best places."

"And I never disappoint. Now, I'm thinking Italian, so why don't you go change into a nice dressy outfit and I'll take you to a great restaurant that you'll never forget. Does that sound okay?"

My arched eyebrow caused him to laugh. "Dressy like a dress?"

"Yes. Is that okay? Do you own a dress?"

Of course I owned a dress. That was a silly question, but I'd never tell him that. "Yup, let me go change. I'll be ready in a few minutes."

He stood straight and leaned back on his desk, but he never took his hand from mine. "Good. I've got a few last details to add to the app and when I'm done I'll meet you in the conference room."

"Okay. See you soon."

He helped pull me to my feet and walked me to the door. As I strode toward the elevator, I refused to look back at him, even though I knew he was watching me. There was no way I wanted him to see the stupid grin plastered on my face, even though he was the one who had put it there.

Chapter 15

With the stupid grin still plastered to my face, I waited for the elevator to take me up, tapping my foot against the dark tile. Since my floor was the next one up, I could have taken the stairs, but with how giddy my body was with the excited energy flowing through it, I would likely trip and hurt myself. I couldn't risk it.

When the elevator doors opened, my eyes fell on a sly grinning Noel who leaned against the wall in the far corner of the small space. She caught sight of me, and her grin grew into a smirk.

"Going up?"

Giddiness drained from me. "Yeah, I am. I'm sorry, but I'm going to have to cancel our girl's night movie."

"Oh I know." My eyes widened at her remark, but either she didn't register my shock, or it didn't bother her. "Merric told me he wanted to take you on a date, so I canceled our plans the moment 'date' left those lips of his. No way was I going to mess with that idea. So you're going up?"

My head nodded like my neck was a limp noodle as I tried to play back what she'd revealed. "Why would he tell you? So you didn't plan on our movie?"

"Nope. It's because he needed me to do some shopping for him. Now, hurry up. You don't have much time. By the way, it's on your bed. Have fun!"

The elevator doors opened onto my floor. For the first time I hadn't noticed the movement of the floor below me. When my feet wouldn't move to turn me around so I could leave the elevator, Noel sprang forward and pushed me out before the doors could close. Rational thought didn't come back until I caught my reflection in the metal of the elevator doors after they'd closed. When it did, I tore down the hallway to my room. What could Merric have wanted her to buy for me when I hadn't even accepted his offer of a date? In fact, I hadn't even known about the date until five minutes ago.

Slowing down before I hit my apartment door at top speed, I slammed the door shut after I'd passed and picked up speed down the hall. I barely made the turn into my room without slamming into the door frame, and skidded to a halt when I caught sight of my bed. Laying on the comforter under a thin, clear plastic protection, was a formal dress.

My fingers itched to touch it, and with care not to hurt the dress, I removed it from the plastic. The burgundy lace of the bodice was smooth under my fingertips as I trailed them over one of the capped sleeves. Without a second's hesitation, I slipped my clothes off and slid into the dress. The entire dress, including the material under the lace, was the same deep burgundy. A built in sash with a tiny bow in the front circled the dress right above my hips where the satin skirt flared out and fell to my knees.

After effectively zipping up the dress, my focus fell on a pair of strappy heels that sat next to where the dress had been. I'd been so focused that I hadn't noticed them until now and I swallowed hard. Back home I'd worn heels, but never ones so high. They would certainly help close the height distance between me and Merric.

With the heels in place, I stumbled to the bathroom to fix my hair and makeup as best as I could. First date jitters had my heart pumping out of control and my hands trembling. Did I tell him this was my first date? Would that turn him off? Probably. Nope, I'd keep that information to myself for as long as possible.

I ran a brush through my hair until the strands were smooth and straight. The green highlights were fading and growing out. I needed to redo them, or I could chop my hair off into a pixie cut. That was worth thinking about, but that thought ended when a soft knock reached me. Did the girl yell for the boy to come inside on a date? No, I needed to answer the door.

With as much grace as a toddler learning to walk, I strutted my way down the hall, keeping my arms stretched out to catch myself when I fell. By some miracle, I reached the door without a twisted ankle. Whatever human invented the stiletto heel deserved a stocking full of coal for the rest of eternity. After taking a few deep breaths, I turned the doorknob to reveal Merric standing on the other side, his fist raised to knock again.

His boyish grin grew as he lowered his hand back to his side and his eyes took me in. "Wow. You look stunning, Holly. Not that you aren't always beautiful, but wow."

With a blush burning my face, I focused on him in his usual white shirt and black pants. Playful courage smothered my sudden shyness as I stepped closed to him to reach out and touch his newest accessory. "A bowtie, huh?"

"You like it?"

"Absolutely. It even matches my dress." I let my thumb run over the silky, burgundy material before he took my hand and placed a kiss to the back of it. My skin heated where his lips caressed and pleasant warmth exploded through my veins.

"Yes, it matches perfectly. Here, before I forget, I have something for you."

From his pocket he pulled a long, thin jewelry box and handed it to me. With shaking hands, I opened it. Lying in the box on a silver chain was a ruby droplet pendent with matching earrings. Gasping, I clapped a hand over my mouth. "Merric, this is too much. I can't accept it." I turned my wide eyes on him and tried to shove the jewelry back at him.

"Yes, you can. No refunds or returns."

"But it's too much."

"No it isn't. Not for you. Come to dinner with me and I'll explain. After I help you with the necklace, of course." He turned my hand so that I still held the box while he removed the necklace and motioned for me to turn around. The jewelry was cool against my skin, and when the necklace was in place, Merric turned me around and took the box from me. "I'll let you handle the earrings."

"Thanks." I took them from where they sat and quickly snapped them in place. "All set. Thank you so much again."

"You are so welcome. They are nothing compared to your beauty, but I do like the way they sparkle, much like your eyes."

I couldn't stop grinning at his cheesy lines. No man had ever spoken to me like that, or given me such a wondrous compliment. For once in a long time, I didn't know what to say, but he saved me from having to say anything.

"Will you be warm enough?"

I glanced down at the sport coat he held draped over his arm and grinned up at him. "I'm from the North Pole, Merric. I should be fine."

"Then let us proceed." He turned while wrapping my arm around his. At least it gave me something to lean on so I didn't shuffle forward like a penguin trying not to face plant. Even better was that he kept his pace slow and steady for me so I wouldn't lose my balance while speed walking.

We didn't meet anyone in the elevator, and the first floor was still fairly empty as elves remained upstairs preparing for tomorrow's baking, or they'd already left for the day. The front desk elves were still in place, and they smiled at us and waved back when I waved to them and called a goodnight.

Outside the air held a slight chill, but it was comforting after the heat of the building. I'd never dreamed I would miss the arctic bite of a snow storm, but more than anything I longed to gather snow in my arms and throw a snowball at the nearest elf, thus starting an epic snowball fight. That went on my to-do list as soon as the first snowflake fell.

"Are you okay?"

Merric's voice pulled me from my thoughts, and I realized I'd stopped walking to bask in the cool evening air. "Yeah, I'm sorry. Was deep in thought. Lead the way."

Stepping toward the curb, Merric hailed a taxi. When one pulled up to the curb and stopped in front of us, Merric opened the door for me and I slid in and across the back seat, and he joined me. After giving the driver an address, he moved to the center seat and reached for my hands as they sat on my lap. He took one and gently squeezed.

"You ready to see the city?"

I nodded and peered out the window as the taxi pulled away from the curb. Soon my face was all but plastered to the window. Merric used this to his advantage and wrapped his arm around my shoulders as he set his face next to mine to stare outside with me.

The buildings were so tall, and the setting sun reflected off the windows of the taller buildings in a dazzling light display. There were more people than I'd ever seen in one place. As we drove, the traffic increased which slowed us down, but that let me see more of the city.

"On the way back, if you're up to it, I want to show you some of the sights. Or would you rather we do that for a second date?" Merric's breath tickled my ear since his face was still so close to mine.

The idea of a second date caused my stomach to flutter. "Let's do that later. It'll be too dark after we eat."

It was a quiet remainder of the ride as I continued to stare in awe out the window. When the taxi stopped, Merric paid him and helped me out. We stood outside a multi story restaurant, and after Merric let me stare a bit, he led me inside. Apparently he'd made reservations because when he told the man standing near the restaurant's entrance his name, we were led to a table on the second floor and seated with menus.

After staring at the menu, I gave up and glanced at Merric, who sat to my right. He'd been offered the seat across from me, but had moved to sit beside me. I loved having him sit so close, especially now that I had a confession to make.

"I have no idea what any of this says. Is it even English?"

Merric chuckled. "It's Italian food, Holly. The names are in Italian, as is much of the menu. What's your favorite Italian dish?"

"I've never had Italian food, at least I don't think I have."

He arched an eyebrow at me. "First you've never eaten pizza, and now you've never eaten actual Italian food. Holly, we need to fix this. I'll order for the both of us. How does that sound?"

"Better than me ordering something I can't pronounce. Do you think they have hot chocolate?" That earned me another laugh.

"Maybe. I can ask."

"Thank you."

"Anything for you, Holly."

A waiter joined us then and asked for our drink preferences. Merric ordered water for both of us and a hot chocolate for me. To my surprise, they were willing to make me some. Since we were also ready to order our food, Merric told him a few dish names I would never be able to remember, and the man left.

"Merric, speaking of anything for me, thank you for the dress and shoes. I ran into Noel. She said you had her purchase them."

He shrugged. "I was busy with a few things that needed my attention, so I showed her a picture of the dress and had her go and buy it. She picked out the shoes. However, I asked her to purchase them. I have no taste in women's shoes."

"But why would you buy me an outfit?"

"Because I hoped you'd say yes to a date, and because I wanted to do something nice for you." He sighed and leaned his elbows on the table. "Most men would have given you flowers, but I hate the senseless killing of a beautiful flower. Plus, they're pretty for a few days and then they shrivel up and die. Why would I want to buy you something that's going to die when I can buy you a perfectly beautiful dress and have the opportunity to see you wear it?"

That was a good reason, at least to me. "Well, thank you again. I can't begin to thank you enough."

"Seeing you wear what I bought is thanks enough, and also having you come to dinner with me. I worried you'd say no."

"Why?"

"Because I'm your assistant. In most work places that's looked down on, but since we aren't most work places, I thought it would be okay."

Before I could respond, the waiter was back with our drinks. Merric took a few swallows from his water glass, and I sipped my hot chocolate. It was amazing, and I moaned while I swallowed the frothy liquid. My date didn't say anything, but I did hear him laugh to himself.

Placing my mug in its place, I turned my attention back to Merric, hoping I could find out more about him. "So, my mom said you went to college. Why would you go to human school?"

He shrugged. "Well, at first it was because my dad wanted me too, and after a while, I began to like it. I liked it enough to choose to attend college, and it allowed me to have the education needed for my position assisting you."

"Is that why your mom's family doesn't like you? Because your dad made you go to human school?"

"Kind of. It's complicated. I promise I'll tell you all about it, but I'd rather not talk about my family issues on our first date. Maybe the second." He winked and sipped his water, thus closing that topic. If he didn't want to discuss it, I'd wait until he was ready.

I gave him what I hoped was a sly look. "Well, if you aren't going to tell me why your mom's family should receive coal for Christmas, why don't you explain why you gave me jewelry and wouldn't take it back? You said you'd explain."

"Ah, that." He chewed his bottom lip while staring out across the room. When he was ready, he turned to me, a pleading gleam in his eyes. "Please don't think of me as a stalker. I'm not, but this may come off kind of stalker-ish."

Any heat I'd been feeling from being near him vanished as a sweeping chill took its place. My father wouldn't have me working with a creeper, would he? I tried to keep the sudden worry that his words gave me from my eyes, but from Merric's frown, I didn't succeed. He shook his head and wiped his hands up and down his face.

"Okay, that came out wrong and was the absolute worst introduction to my explanation."

"Then start explaining," I responded with only a hint of warmth in my voice. "You're worrying me, and kind of scaring me with the term 'stalker.'"

"First, I'm not a stalker, Holly. I give you my word. Anyway, so this story begins last Christmas. Well, before that, but it started coming together last Christmas."

I shook my head at his sudden nervousness that was showing itself through his rapid speaking. "Slow down, Nutcracker. I won't be able to keep up if you keep talking that fast. Start at the beginning and speak slowly, for my benefit."

"Okay, sorry. Here it is."

Chapter 16

"If you don't already know, our mothers are good friends, and have been for years. My mom has talked about you and your sister since I was young, and your mom always sends a Christmas card which my mom hangs on the refrigerator. Well, this past Christmas, your mom sent a family picture along with the card. It was the first time I'd ever seen what your family looks like.

"When I saw you, I was smitten right away. Yes, you're identical to Jolly, but while Jolly has fire in her eyes, yours were as calm as the ocean, and they sparkled. Your smile screamed trickster, but your eyes flowed with goodness. I wanted to meet you right then and there, but I didn't dare say anything to my mother. You're her best friend's daughter, and I didn't want to make it awkward for either one of them.

"But when Chip contacted me about starting this place, I thought maybe I would finally have a reason to visit the North Pole. I never had the chance, though. The day he told me that I wasn't needed up there, he told me one of his daughters would lead the effort here in New York, and I prayed it would be you. So when he told me it would be Holly joining me, I had to bite my tongue until after I hung up. Then I shouted for joy."

He smirked at me and shrugged. "So you see, I'm not a stalker, but it can come across that way, I suppose."

I wasn't sure what surprised me more, that he'd hoped I would be the one to join him, or that he'd seen all of that about me from one picture. Thankfully the waiter chose that moment to bring our food because I had no idea what to say to Merric. Was I pleased he found me attractive? Absolutely. In fact, I loved his description of me.

Merric thanked the waiter before turning his attention back to me. "I think Chip was a bit surprised when I asked him if you were married or spoken for. I blamed needing to know for your apartment, but I was hoping you were single for selfish purposes."

"I've never even been on a date, let alone married," I blurted and squished my eyes shut at my misstep. I'd coached myself not to tell him that on our first date, so why hadn't I listened?

"Hey, it's okay," he laughed, patting my hand before giving it a squeeze. "This just means that I set the bar pretty high for your next date, which will hopefully be us seeing the city, if you still want to do that."

My eyes popped open and I stared at him. "Of course! This is a beautiful city. I want to see it." Especially if I would be living here, and if he was the one showing it to me.

"Good. So you see, Holly, I would do anything for you."

"But why? You don't even know me. Everything you know is from a picture."

He shook his head, chewing the food he'd placed in his mouth. Before he responded, he took a swallow of water. "Do I know you? Yes and no. I want to know you more than I already do, and I do know you, Holly. What I know is that you love Christmas more than anyone else I've met. You are as innocent as you are trouble. And you drink hot chocolate and eat cookies when you're sick, and it helps you feel better. So, no, I don't know you well, but I like what I know, and it keeps me wanting more."

I bit my lip to keep from smiling larger than I should have. "I think that's the nicest thing anyone has ever said to me, especially a boy."

Merric snorted and I arched a surprised eyebrow at him. "Honey, I'm no boy. I'm a man. There's a big difference."

"I'm noticing that," I giggled.

"Good. Now, eat your food. And remember to leave room for dessert. This place has the best chocolate cake."

"Are we allowed to talk about work while we eat?" I asked, sticking the first bite of noodles in my mouth. "Wow, this is even more amazing than it smells."

"First, no we are not mentioning work. And second, this is the best Italian food in the city, at least in my humble opinion."

The waiter came to check on us a few bites later, and brought me another full mug of hot cocoa. With a sigh, Merric asked the man to bring him a cup as well. Merric's response to my questioning grin was to shake his head with a smile and take another bite of pasta.

We kept up a steady conversation throughout the meal, in which I learned he was an only child, loved to watch hockey, and he could play the piano. He'd been living in the city for almost three years, but visited his parents in Maine several times a year. If he hadn't been asked to assist with this project, he would have taken a job in property management. His questions for me were pretty similar, except when he asked about Jolly. Then I made him laugh so hard by telling him some of our pranks he almost spit hot chocolate across the table, but he swallowed in time to save the mess.

After we'd finished our meal, the waiter asked about dessert, which I declined, much to Merric's surprise. "I'm too full, and I don't want to break the zipper in this dress," I explained.

"Then I guess that means I'll have to bring you back here again," he told me after paying for our meal.

"I'm looking forward to it."

The ride home was much the same as the ride to the restaurant. When we stepped from the taxi, Merric took my hand and led me inside. It was amazing to me to be publicly seen with a man who wanted to make a move that would claim me as his girl. Just inside the door, my feet stopped and my good mood ebbed.

"Do you smell that?"

He lifted his nose into the air like it would help him sniff out the scent better. "Smell what?"

"Charcoal. Someone has already burned a pan of cookies and we haven't even officially begun baking yet." I hung my head and took a deep breath. "It's okay, Holly. You've got this. It will all work out."

Merric stood beside me while I coached myself through a near panic attack. Or at least that's what it felt like.

"Holly, what do you do when you're sad or upset?" Merric asked, placing a gentle hand on my shoulder, distracting me from my negative thoughts.

"Well, I usually bake if I'm home. Jolly helps if she's in the mood."

"Okay, well let's bake, and this time I can be your Jolly. Let's make those muffins you wanted to bake a couple days ago. They sounded delicious."

"All right, but I have one condition."

"Anything."

My slow, sly grin had him fidgeting and his eyebrows drew low. "We bake in my apartment."

Relief softened his facial features and he stepped close, placing a kiss on my forehead before I realized his intent. "That sounds like the greatest idea of the day."

"Good. But first I need to find out what burned."

"No, you don't. You need to leave that to the Head Baker and make your muffins."

"Our muffins." With a heavy sigh, I turned toward the elevator. "Come on then, oh assistant of mine. Let's go steal some ingredients."

"You're going to steal ingredients in high heels and a dress?"

His words stopped me before I took a step. He had a point. No way would I be able to hold anything and walk while in these shoes, and there was no way I wanted to soil this gorgeous dress. With any luck, I'd be able to wear it for the bakery's Christmas party. If I was honest with myself, I wanted to wear it a lot, mostly because Merric couldn't take his eyes off of me when I wore it.

"Change of plans. We need to change clothes. I'll meet you back here in fifteen minutes."

"It's going to take you that long to change?" He held up his hands in surrender when I narrowed my eyes at him. "Okay, fifteen minutes. I'll be here."

"Good. And Merric," he turned to me when I said his name, "I like it when you wear jeans."

He smiled wide. "Jeans it is. See you in a few."

Though I loved the dress, the heels were going to take some getting used to. They were killing my feet and I wasn't sure how I made it to my apartment without them causing me any form of bodily harm. The door hadn't even closed behind me before I was attempting to pull the shoes from my feet. When I almost face planted, I gave up and sat on a couch to remove them safely.

Ten minutes later, I was dressed in comfy clothes, complete with fluffy slippers. I was not stuffing my abused feet into any other shoes. When I stepped off the elevator and Merric caught sight of my footwear, his chuckle echoed around the nearly vacant room.

"Nice choice," he laughed, not stopping when he reached me until he was able to bend down and kiss my forehead. "My girl sure knows how to dress for the occasion."

"Of course I do. You're looking pretty comfortable yourself, and is this a Christmas shirt you're wearing?" I tugged on the mentioned shirt, which was made to look like an elf's shirt.

"When in Rome, right?" he asked, spreading his arms for me to take a better look at what he wore.

"What does that mean?"

"Never mind. Let's go steal food to make muffins." He took my hand in his much larger one and led me to the stairs. Since we were only going a couple floors down, there was no use being lazy. Plus, we were headed down, not up.

The storage floors were vacant when we arrived to each, but I was able to point out a few changes that needed to be made, such as making sure flour and sugar spilled on the floor were cleaned up. We did not need rodents in the building, at least Papa had warned me that would happen down here where it was warmer if we let food sit around or we didn't clean up the floor. Beyond that, I wanted a clean building that Santa could be proud to call his.

Loaded down with ingredients, we headed toward the elevator. My prior sickness and fatigue were forgotten as a giddy sense of excitement took their place at the idea of baking with Merric and trying out my new mixer. Since I'd set eyes on it in my kitchen, my fingers had itched to use it. Now I had my chance, and I could also teach Merric about baking.

The ride to my floor was short, and I was bouncing on the balls of my feet by the time the doors opened. Even the elevator ride hadn't bothered me. I was still happy to be free of it, though.

"Come on, Merric," I whined back at him when he stopped to adjust his load.

"You are being impatient," he mumbled with a slight grin on his face. "Thirty seconds won't hurt the muffins."

"You say that now." I waved a wooden spoon at him that I'd taken from the extra storage. "But thirty seconds can mean the difference between a perfectly golden muffin and a burned one."

"Then I guess I was wrong. Lead on, thou who knowest more of baking than I." He gave me a slight bow, succeeding in not dropping any of his load.

Giggling at his silliness, I continued down the hall, and held the apartment door open for him. When he stepped inside, he stopped and grunted.

"Yup, we've got some work to do in here. When we pass Santa's inspection and have a routine down, we'll decorate this place. Compared to the conference room, it is a bit drab." Merric winked at me before striding to the kitchen, with me following behind him shaking my head.

As I gave him instructions, like to turn the oven on to preheat and pull out muffin pans from a tall cupboard across the room, I moved the stand mixer to the center island. While he did as I directed, I found the rest of what we needed, and before I began to measure any ingredients, I waited for him to join me. This was a team effort, and he needed to learn.

Merric joined me when his task was complete and leaned on the counter in front of the recipe, studying it. I didn't need to use it anymore since I had it memorized, but if I was teaching, I needed him to read the recipe.

"Before we start, maybe you can help explain something to me," he stated, staring up at me while continuing to lean against the counter.

"I can try."

"When we started this project and Chip said he wanted regular mixers and items you'd buy for your home instead of larger, industrial sized mixers and equipment used to mass produce, I asked him if that was practical. He said it was necessary. I didn't argue with him or ask questions, but it's been bothering me. Do you know why it's necessary to use the smaller equipment? This project would be much easier using different equipment and we'd need less people."

"Do you remember when we talked about the accounts and how we couldn't lose them because the love that we put in the cookies would be lost to them?" He nodded. "The amount of cookies we can bake, or the muffins we can produce, aren't what's important. Anyone can bake a pie or a fruit cake. What we do is add our love to each individual cookie, muffin, bread, and cake. Each item is individualized and cared for, and the love we put into it while making it is the point of what we do."

"That's why you want the Christmas décor and music. You want that love present in any way you can, not just because you're homesick."

"Yes. If we don't have the love, all we're doing is making cookies."

"And anyone can make a cookie."

"Exactly."

His boyish grin had a troupe of toy soldiers once again parading around my stomach. "Show me how to put love into a muffin."

I handed him a spatula, an egg, and a stick of butter. "It's not something I can show you. It's something you have to feel. You have to care about every aspect of the baking, from cracking that egg to removing a golden muffin from the pan."

He nodded before standing straight and moving close, crowding me against the island before leaning so our faces were inches apart. "Does it help if you care deeply for your baking partner?"

My heart was racing faster than it did every Christmas morning. The heat racing through my veins would have melted a snowman had he come close to me. Merric's eyes melted me, drying my mouth when they dropped to my lips. Did that mean he was thinking about kissing me? Did I want him to kiss me? Stupid question. Of course I did. But would I like it?

He leaned closer, our breath mingling on an exhale, and my eyelids fluttered shut.

Chapter 17

Nothing had prepared me for the emotions and sensations that would accompany my first kiss. Tingling energy ran through my body as time stopped. No cookie or candy cane could taste as sweet as Merric's lips on mine. With gentle tenderness, he deepened the kiss, and I was cookie dough, melding myself to him. His hands slipped to my hips, pulling me closer until our combined heat could have baked the muffins we weren't making.

The blaring screech of the oven finishing preheating made me jump, and I smacked my head against Merric's face, ending our moment. Standing straight, he placed a hand to the spot we'd connected and winced. Under his hand I could already see the skin turning red. Though my head hurt, embarrassment for my reaction pushed the pain aside.

"Oh my goodness, Merric, I'm so sorry! Do you need ice? I'm sorry."

He shook his head, but kept his hand against the wound. "I'm good, Holly. Honest. But thank you for answering my question." Merric's grin and sparkling eyes burned a hole in my chest where my heart thudded against my ribs. "We should go back to baking now or these muffins will never be made."

I wanted to tell him that was fine with me, but I chickened out and turned around to begin the muffin preparations. If there was love floating in the air while we measured, mixed, and baked, it wasn't directed toward the muffins, at least not from me. Every chance we had, one of us was touching the other's hand or standing closer than necessary.

It may not have been love in the air, but it certainly wasn't lust. More like extreme infatuation. By the time the first muffins were baking in the oven, I was barely holding it together. My thoughts kept drifting off to the kiss we'd shared, and my lips tingled remembering the touch of his against mine.

"You're deep in thought," Merric laughed, wrapping his arms around me and pulling me back against his chest. "I hope it's not work related. This was supposed to take your mind off of it."

And it had. Oh had it done that.

With a grin spreading across my lips, I shook my head. "No, definitely not work related."

"Want to tell me what then?"

"Nope."

"Then maybe I'll have to kiss it out of you." The bolder version of Merric turned me to face him, and suddenly shy, I ducked my head. "Oh no you don't."

He lifted my chin with his fingers and lowered his face to mine. My arms wrapped around his neck and his settled on my hips, drawing me closer like he had during our first kiss. This time I was prepared for the effect his kisses had on me, but the longer we kissed, the more intense they grew until I was sure my heart would beat out of my chest.

We were both panting when Merric trailed kisses from my lips to my jaw and up to my temple. Then he kissed both eyelids and the tip of my nose. None of those locations were as stimulating to my hormones, but they allowed us to calm down from our kiss. If this was what all kisses were like, no wonder people liked to buy mistletoe.

I was contemplating stealing another kiss from Merric when the phone in his pocket rang, and he groaned. "That's your father. I told him I'd call today with an update. With everything happening and our date, I forgot to call."

The moment the phone was clear of his pocket, I snatched it from his hand. After verifying it indeed was Papa, I tapped the accept button and lifted the phone to my ear. "Jo Jo's Pizza."

"Holly, is that you?"

"No, sir, this is-," I stared around the room, hoping something would jump out at me. It did in the form of a glass measuring cup. "Crystal."

"Holly." Papa's tone grew gruff, showing his irritation. Merric could only shake his head as he held his hand out for the phone. I didn't give it to him.

"I think you have the wrong number sir."

"Where is Merric?"

"Sir-."

The word barely escaped my mouth before the phone was pulled from my grasp, ending up in Merric's hand instead. "Hello, Chip. Yes, she stole it from me. We're baking muffins, or rather Holly's showing me how."

As he spoke, the timer on the oven beeped, letting us know the muffins were done. I slipped them out of the oven while he watched over my shoulder as I checked that they were done, and set them aside to cool. Papa had a lot of questions, some of which I needed to help Merric answer. Neither of us were prepared for the in-depth interrogation we received, and by the time we were done with Papa, all the muffins were baked and cooling.

"He doesn't miss a thing, does he?" Merric asked after ending the call. He leaned against the counter looking as tired as I felt after the phone call.

"I think that was his way of reminding us to focus. You should head home now. I'll finish cleaning this up and then I'm heading to bed."

He shook his head. "No, I helped make the mess. I can help you clean it."

Swiping the spatula from him that he'd lifted as he spoke, I took his hand and led him toward the apartment door. That he didn't argue with that or try to pull away told me he wanted to go to bed, but he wouldn't admit it to me.

"Go to bed, Merric. It won't take me long, and it'll give me some time to think. And thank you for tonight. It was a great date."

He smiled and pressed his lips to mine in a sweet, short kiss. "It was the best night of my life thus far. I hope there are many more great nights to follow. I'll be following up with you about our next date. But first, let's survive tomorrow, shall we?"

"Don't remind me. I'll see you bright and early."

He squeezed my hand before letting it go to stride down the hall. I watched him turn the corner before closing the door and heading back into the kitchen. The last task I wanted to complete was cleaning up, but Papa would have lectured me from dawn until dusk if he knew I left the kitchen a disaster, especially after letting Merric go for the night.

Once the kitchen was tidy and the muffins placed in air tight containers, I trudged down the hall to my bedroom. It was all I could do to slip on my pajamas and crawl under the covers. Before my mind went completely blank, I remembered to reset my alarm. At least tomorrow I would be waking up on time.

THE FIRST DAY of baking was off to a great start. Nearly every floor had some sort of decoration to brighten the drab room, and elves sang along with every song that played. Rich aromas of baked goods floated in the air, and as I arrived at each floor, I took a deep breath of the new scent that level exuded.

As I floated between floors, elves would call me over to talk and ask questions, both about the product they were making and about Christmas Village. Most of these elves had never lived there or even visited. I texted Merric, who I had yet to see by lunch time, that after the holiday rush, we needed to make a schedule so that each of our elves were able to visit Christmas Village.

It was after a lunch of sugar cookies, pumpkin bread, and milk that the day began to fall apart. First, three separate batches of gingerbread cookies burned to a crisp. All that was left of them were thin, black, indiscernible shapes. In the end, I directed them to just throw the pans away with the inedible cookies. There was no way either item could be salvaged. Apparently the elves whose cookies burnt had been having a dance off and hadn't smelled them burning. I'd smelled them three floors up before racing to the smoke filled floor.

Next, two elves had a disagreement which started a food fight with muffins until the whole of the morning's baking lay scattered across the room. The two that had started the fight were instantly fired by the Head Baker of that floor while everyone else was told to clean up the mess. If I hadn't been so appalled by their destruction of our much needed food, I would have been impressed. They'd used the muffins as I would snowballs, and their aim was just as precise.

A few minutes after the food fight had ended, I sported a muffin sized bruise on my cheekbone that Merric and Noel balked at when they found me helping clean up the mess so the baking could resume. Under Merric's direction, Noel ran for ice while he assisted with the cleanup, keeping a close eye on me since I refused to stop cleaning because of a bruise. When Noel returned with a bag of ice, Merric lifted me onto a stool against my will and shoved the bag in my hand.

"You should have ducked," he commented with a laugh, setting the ice against my cheek.

I winced, and the hand he held at the base of my neck stopped me from pulling away. "I would have, but I'm not used to dodging food. We use snowballs, not baked goods."

"Well, we're short on snow. I'll send out a memo and have several posted in the living quarters that there are to be no more food fights, and that if they need to settle a disagreement, they need to find a new way to do that."

Noel winked at me over Merric's shoulder. "Well, since you're in good hands, I'm going to start fixing my decorations. I'm glad I hadn't finished this floor yet or those two would be coming back to help me."

"Nope, I'm putting them on bathroom duty," I ground out between clenched teeth, waiting for the ice to numb my face. "They're going to keep every bathroom in this place spotless or I'm feeding them to a dragon shifter."

Merric's chuckle tugged a smile at my lips, but the pain in my cheek stopped a wide grin. "Yeah, that could be entertaining. Now, let me go find them and let them know their new duties. You keep that pressed on that bruise. If you don't, I'll know and lock you in your apartment."

I stared around the room and grumbled. My face wasn't the only one bruised, but I was the only person being coddled. Since they'd all been involved with the waste of food, I didn't mention that fact to Merric. However, when Merric disappeared down the stairs, so did the bag of ice. Even when Noel glared at me from across the room, I didn't grab the ice bag again.

"Cherry, what happened here?" I asked the Head Baker of the floor, who was a short, plump, older elf. Her brown and gray hair was pulled back into a tight bun that gave her a no nonsense appearance, but her smile warmed her face. Right now, though, she wasn't smiling. She glared daggers at any elf who dared to glance her way.

"I stepped away to take a bathroom break, and I come back to food flying. If I'd been here, this wouldn't have happened, but I'm older and I needed that break." She frowned deeper at a young elf who'd stopped sweeping to flirt with a young lady. That earned him a muffin to the back of his head. Even Cherry had a strong throwing arm. He winced and continued on his way clearing the floor.

Shaking my head, I returned my attention to Cherry. "You're fine. You should be able to leave the building if you wanted without a fight breaking out. It was irresponsible of them."

"Yes, ma'am, and I'm almost willing to make them all stay until we have twice as much complete as we'd started with, but a tired elf is as bad a baker as a novice elf. We'll do our best to make it up, I promise."

I gave her a warm smile of thanks. "I appreciate that."

"I thought you might."

I was just turning away to continue my tour of the floors when her voice stopped me. "So, you and Merric, aye?"

"Yeah, I guess you could say that." My cheeks heated. It must have been obvious with the way he treated me. That was a first. However, her wary voice cooled me.

"Be careful with that one."

My brows drew low over my eyes as I stared at her. "Why? Is he a bad person?"

She shook her head. "No, not that I know of anyway, but rumor is that his mother married a human, which would make him half human. With how tall he is, it makes sense. Now I don't have a problem with that, but others do. Of course, it's nothing but rumor, but you might want to ask him…or his aunt." Cherry shrugged and sighed. "Anyway, it's none of my business, but I'm happy for you. I'm sure if there was something to worry about, he would have told you by now."

She walked away, and as she did, I let the anxiety that had filled me ease away and I relaxed. She was right. If something like that were true, he would have told me, wouldn't he? He wouldn't have let something that important slip through the cracks without telling me. A marriage between an elf and a human didn't upset me as it did some elves, for whatever reason, but he would have told me.

Leaving that floor, I headed up again to check the progress on the pumpkin and pecan pie level. Since we were still short ovens and the pies weren't needed in the magnitude they would be in another few weeks, we'd chosen to combine them.

Lewis, the floor's Head Baker was chewing out a pair of women for leaving their pies in the oven too long. He held two in his hands, and dismissed them when he saw me. Striding over, he handed me one of the pies he held.

"They look well done," I said, staring down at the overcooked pecans.

"They're done all right. You could use them for hockey pucks. Not even a bird would eat these. The two of them didn't think they were done, so they baked them for twice as long as directed. Now you can't even use a chisel to slice them." Lewis released a gusty sigh and shook his head. "I forget how difficult it can be to train the youngsters."

"But it's worth it, right?"

"Eventually." He winked before spying his next victims and bid me farewell.

At least this floor appeared under control, if you didn't count the two rock hard pies. There were still several levels to inspect, but my head and muscles were growing tired. Noel found me as I debated going upstairs for a short reprieve. She wore a wide grin and I wasn't sure if I should stay and say hi or run.

Chapter 18

"There you are! I was hoping you wouldn't go too far," Noel laughed, wrapping her arms around my shoulders and squeezing tight until I squeaked. "Now, are you ready to have some fun?"

Fun? Now?

"Noel, I'm working," I told her, omitting that I'd been thinking of slipping in a quick nap.

"This is fun and working, I promise. You look like you need a break, and I want some help. C'mon!" Noel grabbed my hand and dragged me toward the elevators. She repeatedly slammed her thumb against the door close button after punching the button for the first floor.

"Where are we going?"

"Shopping. I need supplies and an opinion. And you need a break. Merric said you're grinding your teeth in frustration, and I told him I had the perfect way to relax you."

Merric had noticed me grinding my teeth? When had he noticed that? If it was when he held the ice to my face, there was a reason for the grinding: pain. Thankfully my cheek was no longer throbbing, though I was sure that I still wore a bruise.

The elevator doors hadn't even opened completely before Noel was dragging me after her toward the building's main entry. As always, the office staff elves waved or called a greeting. My response barely left my lips before a bitter blast of wind stole my breath as I followed my kidnapper outside. That's what she was, stealing me away from my job.

"I should've grabbed my coat," Noel muttered, releasing my hand to wrap her arms around herself. Once I'd faced the initial shock of the cold, I'd quickly acclimated to the bitter weather. In another few weeks

I would need a coat outside. At a certain point, cold was just cold, no matter how chill the temperature.

"You could always buy one while we're out," I suggested, letting her lead by half a step.

"Not in this city. Have you seen the prices? I'll suffer for today. Next time, I'll swing by my apartment and grab my jacket before we head out. So, now that we're away, tell me about yourself." Noel skirted a pile of trash to rejoin me.

The crowd around us was growing, and several of the humans cast us questioning and odd gazes before continuing on their way. To them, we appeared to be little more than children, and short at that. However, my ID that Papa had given me clearly stated I was eighteen. Eighteen and running the only Christmas bakery in operation. Yes, Papa was crazy for trusting me with that.

"There's not much to tell, really. I grew up in Christmas Village, and this is the first time I've left. My best friends are my twin sister and a dragon shifter named Vixen. She just found her mate, so they've been busy moving into their house. And Jolly's found a new job, but because I won't tell her what's happening with Merric, she won't tell me what it is. That's pretty much our relationship. We're also adept at bouncing between the Naughty and Nice Lists." She arched an eyebrow at me and I shrugged. "We never took life too seriously. Your turn. Tell me about you."

She dodged a man who wasn't paying attention and I skittered around a man selling who knew what. Was this part of the city safe? If not, I was sure Merric would have joined us.

"I grew up in Texas, actually. My parents loved it there when they visited, so that's where they stayed to raise us. I'm sure it's different for you here, living among humans, that is. For me, it's normal. Dad's a tinkerer so he makes one of a kind toys for Santa. Mama sews stuffed animals for local hospitals. Me…I haven't quite figured out my niche in life. Maybe this is it." She grinned wider, a twinkling sparkle in her eyes.

"You mean living at the bakery and decorating?"

"More the decorating. I'm thinking that after this, I might look into being an interior Christmas designer."

In her excitement, Noel picked up her pace, and I fought to keep up. "Is there such a thing?"

"Who knows, but nothing says I can't try. Here, let's try this place." She indicated a store on our right where a human man was changing out the front window display for one that was Christmas themed.

Inside we were met with decorations of all kinds. Even though Halloween and Thanksgiving were still looming on the horizon, a corner of the store had already begun to stock Christmas décor. A giddy squeal escaped me, and I tried to smother it behind my hands, but I hopped from foot to foot when I stared at all of the gorgeous ornaments, decorations, and dishes.

"What's our budget?" I asked when I could form words again.

"And I quote: 'Don't go too crazy.'" She laughed at my mouth open, wide-eyed stare. "Merric's words, not mine. He messed up when he added the 'too' in the middle of that statement. It leaves the limits wide open. You see, my definition of 'too crazy' and his are very different, but I'm the one shopping, so my definition is the one that counts. Now, what do you like? I have a rule when doing this: we don't leave any store empty-handed."

"Seriously?"

Noel shrugged. "You bet. So, pick something."

"Do you have themes for each floor? Or just going with whatever fits?"

Her eyes met mine with a wild twinkle as she smirked. "I knew we'd be great friends. Yes, I have themes, at least for the floors that are finished. Right now I'm trying to find decorations for a winter wonderland and peppermint themed floors. To keep my mind from becoming a rat's nest of ideas, I'm searching for a few floors at a time instead of the whole enchilada."

"Good plan."

My eyes scanned across the decorations, and with care, I strode up and down the designated Christmas aisles. At one point Noel caught me and told me not to forget my apartment, that if there was anything that caught my eye that I wanted, I was to let her know so she could purchase it. After sneaking a peek at a few price tags, I swallowed hard and decided not to look again.

"Noel," I called, and she joined me a few seconds later. "Why don't you take some of these red and white striped ornaments and stick them in some fancy glass dishes and place them on any counters or shelves that might be unoccupied on your peppermint floor?"

Her grin grew. "That's brilliant. I can even throw some candy canes in a few others to change it up a bit too."

"That would be great for a hot chocolate bar on each floor," I gushed, grabbing her shoulders and shaking her slightly in my excitement, but with her growing smile, it didn't appear she minded my manhandling.

"That's brilliant! Okay, so you're better at this decorating thing than I am, but that's okay. You've got tips and a new way of approaching the ideas. I like it."

My eyes rolled. "Noel, I'm from Christmas Village. What I suggest is only what I've already seen. Girl, before you become a professional decorator, you have to visit Christmas Village. It's a must for you."

She squealed and hopped on her toes, drawing some attention our way, but I ignored the stares. We were excited. Noticing some fake evergreen wreaths hanging above us, I narrowed my gaze. Noel stopped her hopping and followed my stare.

"Let me guess, you're thinking of a wreath level?"

I shrugged. "Or evergreen. Like this wreath, but also garland as well. Maybe with red bows. Although, a wreath level isn't a bad idea either."

"Merric is going to flip out when he sees what we're going to bring home."

My eyebrows shot halfway up my forehead. "You honestly think we can carry all of what you want to buy?"

Her crooked smile gave her a wicked appearance. "Nope, but I have my team on speed dial. Let me give them a call and we'll start picking everything out. If you aren't aware, we only have eight days left until the deadline. That means I have seven days to have that place in tip top shape and fully decorated, minus the floors that aren't being used yet."

Whistling, I shook my head as my stare went back to the decorations around us. "You're right. Merric is going to flip. I'm blaming you.

He knows what I'm like, and that it would be a bad idea to take me shopping like this without a budget."

"What he doesn't know won't hurt him. Yet."

While we waited for Noel's team, we picked out evergreen boughs and various wreaths, glass jars, and a few stylishly decorated Christmas mugs. To keep our bill reasonable, we decided to place a hot chocolate station every three floors instead of on every floor. Eventually there would be one on every floor, but even I didn't want to push Merric's level of spending acceptance, especially when I didn't know where the money came from, whose it was, or how much was left. A few human employees were recruited to assist us with items we couldn't reach. When the team appeared, Noel paid for what we'd already set aside and sent them back with those items while we finished shopping. Since we only chose a few other random items, including a cute cookie plate for my apartment and a fancy glass tree for my office, Noel let her team know they didn't need to come back.

Darkness was descending on us when we finally left the store, but it didn't dampen our moods. It had been a great end to my day, especially after all of the incidents. Refusing to think about that, I opened my mouth to ask Noel about her favorite Christmas traditions, but she beat me with her own question.

"How are you doing with your job anyway? And I don't want answers like 'Good' or "Fine.' I want details."

I eyed her carefully, scanning her face for an ulterior motive. "You aren't going to report back to Merric, are you?"

"Nope, this is me being a friend. You've been sick and you've been dealing with a bunch of baking elves who have no idea what they're doing. It has to be tiring and stressful."

"Down right exhausting."

She flashed me a grin. "And that's why I asked. Anything I can do to help?"

"Just keep making our work environment a Christmas wonderland. We'll be fine. It's going to take longer than I expected to be fully up and running but we can manage."

"Yes, we can. We just have to keep working as a team. By the way, speaking of teams," she nudged me with her hip, "how are you and

Merric doing? Did he like the dress on you? Please tell me he did because if he didn't, I may have to question his intelligence."

Heat rushed to my face, neck, and even my ears. "Yes, he liked the dress. I think I almost rendered him speechless."

"Well, good. At least he's got a good brain between his ears." She wiggled her eyebrows at me. "How was dinner? Did it taste good?"

From the glint in her eyes, I wondered if she wanted to ask me if *he* tasted good. The answer to both questions was an absolute yes, but I would never admit that. Not yet anyway.

"It was delicious. He took me to an Italian restaurant. I may have eaten way too much. Then we came back here and baked muffins in my apartment."

Her grin grew. "Then what?"

"Then he left. What?" I was more than a bit edgy from her smile, and every alarm in my head told me to run for it.

"You're killing me. Didn't he kiss you or you kiss him or something? If not, I'm going to smack you both. Everyone can see how infatuated you two are with one another. Seriously, girl."

My blush deepened, and I turned away from her, but not in time. Noel gasped and grabbed my shoulder before squealing. "Shut up! You did kiss, didn't you? Oh come on, girl, don't leave me hanging. Why didn't you tell me? That should have been the first words out of your mouth when we stepped outside. Come on, I want details."

"Noel! Calm down," I told her, waving my hands to keep her quiet. She'd attracted attention from passersby, and this wasn't something I wanted to share with the strangers of New York. "Yes, we kissed. Yes, I liked it. And yes, it was everything I'd ever hoped my first kiss would be. Now will you calm down?"

"Absolutely not! You can't tell me all of that without giving details."

"Oh yes, I can. They're private. All you need to know is that we kissed, twice if you must know, and then Papa called and we spent the next part of eternity answering his questions."

"Wait, you answered the phone on your date?" Noel's smile fell and she glowered at me. "Date protocol says you don't answer your phone when on a date. You focus on your date."

"Well, it was late, and Merric had forgotten to call Papa, so Papa called him. It was necessary, and the date was basically over anyway." Although, I could have enjoyed a few more kisses if Papa hadn't called.

"Whatever. I don't agree with it, but what's done is done. Did he ask you out for a second date?"

We were approaching the building, and I slowed so I could answer the question before we stepped inside. Rumors already flew around the bakery staff. I didn't need to add to them by discussing my relationship in a room that echoed. That was asking for trouble.

"We're going on a second date, but I don't know when. He wants to show me around the city more. Now, this subject is closed until we are in private, okay?"

She eyed the inside of the building and nodded. "Yup. And we're about to face your boyfriend's wrath if his stare and body language are accurate."

I followed her stare inside to see Merric standing in the middle of the room, arms crossed over his chest, watching us cross in front of the building to the doors. He wasn't glaring at us, but he wasn't smiling either. It was a hard stare, and his eyes narrowed when we entered the building and he caught sight of the few bags we carried.

Instead of cowering under his stare like I wanted to, I strode right up to him and gave him my biggest, brightest smile. "I needed this."

His eyes softened at my words, and he slipped the bags from my hand to his. "I know, but let's try and keep the spending under control. We don't have to buy an entire store every day." His gaze drew to Noel, but flew back to me when I poked him in the stomach.

"It was all my ideas. Noel just went along with them." I briefly hesitated. "Did we overspend?"

He shook his head. "No, at least Santa hasn't given me a spending cap…yet." Merric eyed Noel again, who laughed.

"I'm going to sort through what we bought. If you two need me, I'll be in my office." Noel headed toward the row of private offices. She's claimed one as her office, and everything she bought ended up there before she placed it. That left me alone with Merric since the office staff had left for the day.

"Are you mad?" I whispered to him, regaining his attention when he watched Noel leave, shaking his head at her.

"At you? No. I like giving Noel grief, mostly so she doesn't buy an entire store."

I tugged his shirt until he bent and pressed his lips to mine in a sweet kiss. "Then you should have given her a budget," I teased, earning myself another kiss.

"I'll remember that. Now, how about we try out those muffins we made while checking out today's progress on the first order?"

"That sounds like a brilliant idea."

Chapter 19

Merric ate three muffins before we left my apartment, and before I'd finished one. If I had to guess, he had a much larger sweet tooth since we first met. I took the credit for that when he dug through my fridge to find the milk and filled us both a glass to cut the sweetness from the muffins.

He led me down the halls to the elevator, stole a kiss inside, and motioned me out of the elevator before him. Elves in the packaging department, which was located on the first floor opposite the main entrance, were hard at work boxing cookies, pies, cakes, and muffins for the first order. Some caught us watching them and smiled, but most were too busy boxing and packing to notice two stragglers moving between the set up tables they worked at.

Jewel stood in the middle of the room, directing the elves where to place their completed boxes as she made notes of what items were prepared. When she noticed us approaching, she smiled, directed her current employee where to put a boxed pumpkin pie, and turned to us. Her smile widened at our clasped hands before she nodded.

"I heard rumors. I'm glad to see they were correct."

We smiled back at her, and Merric squeezed my hand. "Yup, this one is true. Not all of them are."

Jewel nodded before turning to direct a few elves where to place their goods. When she again gave us her attention, she was scribbling notes on the paper attached to her clipboard. "Well, we're almost a quarter done with this order. If we don't have problems tomorrow like I heard we had today, we should almost complete the order, but most likely it'll be finished in two days. You might want to send down the next order form so I can start placing it as well," she directed Merric, who nodded at her.

"I'll do that first thing in the morning. If I don't, I'll forget."

"If you do, I know where to find you." Jewel winked at me. "Now, I'm going back to work. Don't snitch anything," she warned us.

"Don't worry, we ate some muffins before we came down to tide us over," I reassured her, and she nodded.

"I'll likely eat a few more when we're finished here," Merric muttered under his breath before breathing in deeply of the rich smells surrounding us. I couldn't have agreed more when my stomach rumbled. Jewel eyed me with a warning stare and I dragged Merric away before food did go missing.

He walked me back to my room, we ate a few more muffins, and then he left for the night with a promise to see me in the morning. His evergreen scent stayed with me after he kissed me and closed the door behind him. I was just heading to change into my pajamas and crawl under the covers for an early night when my phone buzzed in my pocket. Papa's number came up, but I wasn't sure who would be on the other end.

"This had better not be Jolly." My greeting was met with a gusty groan.

"Seriously, Holly? That's how you answer the phone? Didn't Papa teach you any manners?"

My grin widened into a smile. "Hello, Jolly."

"Hello yourself. Now, tell me what's going on. I miss you!"

I flopped on a couch and stared up at the ceiling, debating what to tell her. Since she was going to find out anyway, I settled on the truth. With a last second thought, I took the receiver away from my ear so she wouldn't deafen me if she screamed.

"Well, Merric kissed me."

"What!" she shrieked, just like I knew she would. Even with the phone held away from my ear, it still hurt. "When? What happened? Start at the beginning, you little snot. What else am I missing?"

Closing my eyes, I reveled in the joy of the last few days with Merric. In great detail, I shared with her about our time together, our date, and baking muffins. I did not give details about the kiss, no matter how much she prodded or threatened me. Some things were just too personal.

"You really like him, don't you?" Jolly asked, a wistful air to her voice. "I can see your silly grin from here when you talk about him."

"I wish you were here," I confided, my smile slipping for the first time since we started talking. "I miss you so much, and you always know what to say. You could give me your opinion of him, although that might also be a bit scary."

"Hey!"

"But you'd be able to help me know I'm doing everything right."

She sighed into the phone. "Well, from the sound of it, you don't need me there to be doing something right. If he's still fawning over you after you spent an evening together, then he's hooked. Tell him if he hurts you I will shave his head."

Now it was my turn to groan and slap my hand across my face. Of course she'd end her statement with a threat. However, I knew Jolly well enough that if Merric did hurt me, Jolly really would shave his head. Only she had to leave the North Pole first.

"Fine, I'll tell him," I moaned, "but you stay away from him if he's being nice."

"Of course."

"And when you find an elf, the same applies."

"Deal."

My eyes narrowed, even though she couldn't see them. "Is there an elf, Jolly?"

Her lips buzzed on an exhale. "No, not really. There's this one guy I like, but I'm pretty sure he's not interested in me. Sparkle says you shouldn't have to chase them if they're into you, so I backed off. She's probably right anyway."

"Yeah, I'll agree with that. I'm sorry, Jolly."

"Don't be. You have your man, and that's what's important. I'll be fine. Between you and Vixen, I'll be busy being Aunt Jolly."

Rolling my eyes, I sat up, a yawn escaping me. "Jol, I'm not even engaged. This may not turn into anything permanent. Quit planning my wedding."

"Too late. I already picked out your bridesmaids dresses."

"Jolly!"

Her laugh cut me off. "Relax, Holly. I haven't done anything. I promise."

"Like you promised Papa we hadn't done anything for April Fool's Day?"

I could almost hear the cringe in her voice. "Nope, nothing like that. He already knew we'd done something. No, this is different. I won't plan anything until you tell me to."

Still unable to believe her, I dropped the subject. "What's happening there? What job have you taken?"

"Umm, can I tell you that in person the next time I see you? I want to see your reaction, not just hear it."

Okay…

"That could be a while."

She corrected me with great haste. "Actually, Papa and Mama are bringing me with them to see you at the Grand Opening."

"If there is one. I'm still trying to ship the first order out. It wasn't the greatest of days in the bakery."

"Tomorrow can't be worse, can it?"

"It absolutely could."

Jolly giggled. "But it could also be better. Now, I'm heading to bed. I love you, sis."

"Love you too, Jolly. Tell Mama and Papa hello for me and that I love them."

"Will do."

After she hung up, I stared out over the city for a few minutes before dragging my attention back to the apartment. Turning on the TV to a station playing Christmas music, I went to my room, changed, and crawled into bed. It was a blessed relief to fall asleep to music again. Tomorrow night I would play it on the TV in my bedroom so I could hear it better.

THE EARLY NIGHT to bed had been a great idea, and I woke up more refreshed than I had since arriving in New York. Merric was already typing away at his computer when I entered his office without knocking. Well, since he had the door wide open, I didn't see a reason to knock. Seeing him behind his desk made me wonder if my office would ever be used. So far I hadn't spent much time in it. Maybe once we were up and going and I could trust the goings on below, I would take more time to work there.

Merric continued typing, oblivious to my watchful gaze. His fingers flew across the keyboard in a way mine had never done. It would take hours of practice to achieve his swift perfection. Even his eyes never left the screen as he typed. However, I could tell when he made a mistake. The skin around his eyes crinkled until he fixed the error, and then he continued like nothing had happened.

"Mind if I interrupt?" I asked, and giggled when he leapt in his seat. He rested a hand over his heart and took a few deep breaths, shaking his head.

"I don't mind, if you don't scare me like that again."

"No promises," I told him, settling myself in the uncomfortable looking chair I'd sat in the last time I was in his office. "Now, what are your plans for the day?"

He rolled his chair away from the computer so that he was sitting across from me, leaning over the desk. "Well, I'm sending Jewel the next two orders as we speak before I forget and she comes head hunting. Then I thought I'd grab the inventory forms from your office, find you, and help you enter in the information for an order. It'll be a small one, but at least you'll know how to do it for next time. After that, I thought I'd start organizing the employee files in your office, if you're okay with that," he hedged, motioning to several stacks of papers and folders that sat on a square table behind his chair.

"That's fine. You can go in my office any time you want. Do you want help?"

"Only if you want to give it. It's nothing difficult. More boring than anything, but it's necessary."

I nodded, understanding that statement. "Well, when I'm done in the bakery today, I'll come find you and help you finish."

"Good. Now, why don't I join you for breakfast? I heard Noel say something about a hot chocolate bar on the first floor. Apparently it's the only one set up so far." He stood, walked around his desk, and led me from his office with a hand on the small of my back. His warm fingers brushed against my shirt as he kept his hand pressed against me when we neared the elevators.

"You forgot something." I smirked at him, lifting my eyes to him, batting my lashes lightly. His eyes narrowed at my statement.

"I did?"

"Of course. Where's my good morning kiss?"

Dawning lit his face and his eyes gleamed as he wrapped his arms around my waist and mine went around his neck. This was no swift kiss as he preferred when we were either in a hurry or in a more public setting. This kiss was slow and sweet, warming me from my core to my fingertips and toes. The ding of the elevator arriving didn't jolt us apart, but the tinkling laugh that echoed around the empty floor did.

Our lips broke apart, but Merric pulled me closer to him, and slightly behind him until he realized our threat was none other than Noel. The elevator was packed with her decorating supplies, and she stood in the midst of them, hiding a giggle behind her hands. Merric ran a hand through his spiky hair before wiping his face with it.

"Not funny," he muttered, leading me toward the elevator. "What are you doing up here anyway?"

"I was looking for Holly to ask if she wanted to help me decorate, but I see she was busy." Noel winked at me, and I grinned wider instead of blushing. If it had been anyone else who'd caught us, I would have been beet red. However, Noel was reminding me in some ways of Jolly, so she was more sister than friend at this point.

"Sorry, Noel," I laughed, "but I'm working with the Head Bakers on the floors I didn't reach yesterday, at least until Merric finds me for a computer training session."

"Yup, I'm sure it'll be quite a training," she teased, and he ignored her as he stared at her various wreaths and garlands.

"Oh stop. Maybe I can find some time tomorrow to help you."

"Good. We'll go shopping again. I can use some more of your ideas."

Merric peered up from his study to give us both a hard stare. "You two aren't allowed to go shopping alone together again. Plus, Holly is busy tomorrow night."

"Oh, I am? Doing what?" I asked him as we reached the first floor and the doors opened.

"Taking a tour of the city."

My heart leapt. Our second date. Merric's eyes sparkled, and I was sure mine matched with anticipation of spending another night out together…alone.

Noel cleared her throat, breaking us out of our trancelike stare. Merric's grin grew into a smirk before he led me from the elevator, allowing Noel to ride back up to her desired floor. Her giggling followed us until the doors closed.

The room was jammed full of elves, everyone waiting for their turn at the hot chocolate station. Merric and I groaned at the same time and eyed one another. Without waiting for him to move, I punched the elevator button so that I could rejoin Noel. I was reassigning her first task to be setting up a hot chocolate station on every floor we'd discussed. At this rate, elves would start baking by mid afternoon to early evening.

"This is going to be a mess." Merric stood beside me, surveying the scene before us.

While we waited, I nudged him. "Can you whistle above the noise in here?"

Nodding, he placed two fingers in his mouth and released an ear splitting whistle that startled everyone into a silence that hung over the room like a blanket. Every head turned my way. I should have been nervous with so many elves staring at me, but annoyance had taken the place of nerves.

"Listen up, everyone. You will all go to your designated floors and begin baking. One floor at a time will be dismissed to come down and have a hot chocolate break. Beginning tomorrow, every third floor will have hot chocolate available, and you will use the station closest to your floor. However, if you abuse the privilege, you will be banned from taking a hot chocolate break. Instead, you'll get water. Now, head upstairs. Thanks."

A few grumbles by those closest to the hot chocolate filled the air, but otherwise the room was quiet except for shuffling feet. No one wanted to argue and lose hot chocolate privileges. I didn't blame them.

Merric had already restocked the hot chocolate mix in my apartment. It reminded me to have Jolly sneak some to me from Christmas Village when she came for the Grand Opening.

The elevator opened and a group of us filed in, heading to the upper floors. Since I'd already had my cup this morning, I exited with those on the top most baking level while Merric continued back up to his office. It saddened me we hadn't been able to spend a bit more time together, but if I hurried with today's tasks, I could join him sooner.

Taking a deep breath, I followed the elves toward the Head Baker's table, ready to assist again and hoping that today would prove better than yesterday. If another food fight ensued, I would be rethinking my forms of punishment to keep it from happening again.

Chapter 20

Jewel found me minutes before my quitting time to inform me we had completed the first order. I let her know I'd tell Merric so we could have it shipped out right away to make room for the next order. It was a blessed relief to have one order heading out, and ahead of her forecasted schedule. With no food fights to deplete the day's work, we'd managed to make good headway. In fact, it was an overall much better day than the one before. A few pans of cookies were a touch burnt, and some muffins had overflowed their wrappers, but otherwise it had been a productive day.

Relief swamped me as I made my way up to my office. Merric had found me mid morning with my hands dirty up to my elbows while I assisted a pair of elves clean up their station for the next batch of cookies. Somehow, they'd managed to spread a coat of flour all over their work station. He stayed long enough to mention doing training another time and left, keeping a wary eye on me.

A startled squeak escaped me before I smothered it when the elevator doors opened and Carol stood just on the other side of them. She didn't even crack a smile at the sound, but her frown deepened when she stepped aside to let me pass. We bid one another a quick hello and goodbye before I scurried up the hall to put distance between us. She'd at least had a smile for me yesterday when I'd worked on her floor.

Merric wasn't in any better of a mood, and I quickly dismissed myself from helping him with his project. The two had obviously had words, and none of them good. The hurt glint in his eyes caught my attention when I told him I'd see him later, but I couldn't stay around him when I wasn't sure how he'd react. His words had been clipped and his nostrils had flared several times. Even a drawer had suffered his wrath when he'd slammed it back into the file cabinet.

I was midway through a pint of ice cream while watching the city skyline when a light knock sounded at my door. Without peering through the peep hole, I knew it was Merric. The cadence of his knocking rarely changed much, and only he and Noel would come to see me at this time of night. Setting the ice cream down on an end table, I stood to let him in.

His mournful gaze met mine the moment the door was open so he could peer inside. He didn't move to come in, and I didn't step back to let him. I needed to know what type of mood he was in first.

"I'm sorry for the way I acted. It was wrong," he stated, stepping forward ever so slightly, bringing him closer to me. "I think I scared you, and I'm sick to my stomach at the thought. I'd never hurt you, Holly."

"Is that why you took it out on the file cabinet?"

He tried not to smirk by tucking his lips into his mouth and biting down on them. While he composed himself, I waited for my answer. I didn't see anything funny about it.

When I remained silent, he finally spoke up again. "Yes, I closed the drawer with more force than I should have, but that's usually pretty normal for me. There's something about a drawer slamming shut that I like. Today I closed them a bit too hard. Are you upset because I slammed the drawers shut?"

I fought not to roll my eyes, and barely succeeded. "No, you were upset and I didn't know how to act around you. I was worried you might yell at me or something." Tugging at the hem of my shirt, I dropped my gaze to the floor. With my eyes averted, I didn't see him move until he reached me, wrapping me in a tight hug.

"Holly, I'm so sorry," he whispered into my ear. "I never meant to cause you worry like that. Please forgive me. I promise to behave better next time I'm upset, which doesn't happen often."

"What did Carol say that upset you?" I asked from deep inside his embrace. That close to him, I felt him stiffen.

"Nothing that I want to discuss now. I'll explain more about our family dynamic later. It can be a bit…tense."

"Can you two work together?"

"Yes." He released me and backed up a step, meeting my eyes as he did. "Are we good? Or do I actually need to beg you to forgive my bad mood and the way I treated you?"

Technically he hadn't treated me poorly, just the file cabinets. I'd retreated when his black mood had appeared mildly volatile without actually giving him a chance to explain himself. I shouldn't have condemned his behavior before he'd acted poorly against me. If we were to make this relationship work, we needed to learn to communicate.

"There's nothing to forgive, not yet anyway. You weren't mean to me, but you needed some time to cool down. I was just giving it to you."

He shook his head. "I scared you enough to think I would yell at you. That was wrong."

Reaching my hand up around his neck, I pulled his face down to mine and placed a soft kiss against his lips. "Then yes, I forgive you for scaring me. Next time, talk to me and tell me you're all right, or a bit upset. Don't leave me guessing if you're mildly annoyed or ready to blow a fuse."

Laughing, he kissed me back. "All right. I can do that. I'm finished in your office, and I wanted to clear the air between us before I headed to bed. I've had a long day, so I think I'm going to call it an early night. Plus, my mom has been calling all day and I haven't answered. I need to call her back before she thinks I'm lying dead somewhere and calls Aunt Carol to make sure I'm alive."

"Call your mom," I directed and placed a goodnight kiss to his lips. He groaned when I pushed against his chest for him to release me before deepening the kiss until I stopped pushing at him. When we were both panting, he broke the kiss off and placed another against my forehead before bidding me goodnight and closing the door after himself.

Now that I was satisfied we were okay, I covered my ice cream, set it back in the freezer, and headed to bed. After a successful day, I hoped tomorrow would go just as well.

. . .

The next day began like any other day thus far, and again I moved floor to floor to check on the progress. Everyone was growing used to their assignments and had fewer questions and concerns. At least questions about the work. More elves asked me personal questions, which allowed me to ask them in return and get to know the bakers. However, it also left me open for questions about Merric. More than one of the few people who brought him up mentioned the possibility of human blood in his family. With every comment, I began to grow ever more curious about what he was hiding when he spoke of his family's situation and the problems they had.

By midday I'd had enough of those comments and went straight to the second source of the information I sought. Since Merric wasn't telling me, and I wasn't sure how to ask him, I went in search of his Aunt Carol, hoping she'd be more willing to talk to me. When I exited the elevator on the gingerbread cookie floor, I moved straight to the Head Baker station. Carol wasn't hard to spot since no one surrounded her area, and she was replenishing her stock.

"What can I do for you?" she asked a bit tersely when she spotted me approaching.

"Can we talk for a minute? Somewhere private?" It appeared everything was under control on this floor, as it should have been. When elves had been assigned, they'd placed most of the experienced bakers on this floor because of the details required to cut and decorate the cookies.

Her eyes narrowed a fraction, but she nodded and called another elf over to sub in for her while she was gone. I strode across the floor back to the elevator with Carol on my heels. Even when we were alone in the elevator, we didn't speak.

I pressed the numbered button for one of the vacant levels, and when we arrived, walked into the room. Since the stairway was near us, I led Carol across the floor until we were far enough away I hoped no one would hear us. When I stopped, so did she, and before I could say anything, she began grouching at me.

"If Merric said anything about me being unprofessional and not keeping a distinction between work and personal life, then he lied. I made sure he knew that our conversation yesterday was strictly personal, and not work related. Since I was off the clock, it doesn't classify as work time."

I held up a hand to stop her, and was pleasantly surprised when she stopped talking.

"Merric didn't say anything. This is me wanting to talk to you in an off the record conversation. I don't know what you two talked about yesterday, and I don't care to know. What I do want to know," I hesitated briefly, then spat the words out, "is Merric half human?"

Her eyebrows shot up her forehead before a smirk tugged at her lips. "Well, I must admit I'm a bit surprised you're asking me that instead of him."

I shrugged. "Well, if he is, that explains why every time his family is mentioned, he shuts the conversation down and refuses to talk about it. Not that I care if he is or if he isn't, but I want to know."

She nodded and sighed, crossing her arms over her chest. "I told him to tell you everything or I would. He didn't take that well, as you saw last night. It would be best if he told you his secrets, so don't mention speaking to me at all. And I would talk to him now, and if I were you, I'd be as direct with him as you were with me. He needs to know how important it is for you to know the truth from him, not everyone else." Without waiting for me to respond since my brain was still digesting what she said, Carol turned on her heel and made her way back to the elevator.

I stood in numb silence, watching as she stepped inside and the doors closed behind her. Was she saying that Merric was half human, or was there another larger secret I didn't yet know about? However, she was correct. I needed to find out from him, and the more I thought about it, the more irritated I became that he hadn't yet been honest with me. Didn't he trust me?

Sprinting to the stairs, I climbed the next few flights to reach Merric's all but empty floor. His door stood open again, so as always, I stepped inside without knocking. This time he glanced up from papers on his desk to smile at me, but it faltered when he caught my hard stare. I tried to calm down as I closed the door to keep our conversation private, but my agitation remained.

Merric sat quiet and still when I turned back to face him, though he played with a pen in his hands. His eyes never left me, and I placed my hands on my hips, refusing to step any further into the room. I had to know the truth before I could make myself comfortable.

"What is it Holly?" he asked when I remained silent. For some reason, now that the moment was here, I couldn't make my jaw work. A part of me wanted to know the truth, and another part of me that did know it already was breaking because he hadn't trusted me enough to tell me the truth.

"Are you half human?"

His eyes widened before they narrowed. "Did Aunt Car-."

"Your beloved aunt only told me one thing, and that was to talk to you. Now man up and fess up."

With a long, drawn out sigh, Merric rubbed his brows, closing his eyes before letting his head fall forward. "Yes, my mother is an elf and my father is a human."

"You should have told me," I accused, my voice quivering with my anger, frustration, and disappointment. "For days I've been asked if you are or if you aren't. Some have speculated that you are and have asked me how I could date someone like you. Others ask me what it's like to date a half human elf. And do you know what I have to say about that? Nothing! Or I can tell them we haven't talked about it, or that I'm not even sure you are half human. They stare at me like I'm insane and either walk away or awkwardly change the subject.

"Merric, what you are doesn't bother me. What bothers me is that you never bothered to trust me enough to tell me. Were you ever planning to tell me? You've had how many chances, good chances, to do so and every time you tell me we'll talk about it later. Well, later is here, and it's far past time. I should not have to come to you and ask you to tell me the truth."

After my tirade finished, he remained still. A tiny piece of guilt ate at me for being so blunt and spewing out words without censoring them, but my hurt squashed it. The words may have been blunt, but they were all true. The almost yelling delivery of them could have been handled better, but it appeared he got the point.

Without a word, Merric stood and rounded the corner of his desk. Before he could wrap his arms around me like he wanted, I placed my hand against his chest and pushed him back slightly. He let his arms drop to his side, defeated.

"Yes, Holly, I should have told you. I wanted to so badly, but my fear overruled my trust. You don't know what it's like to be made fun of your whole life like I have been. Elves laugh because of my father's blood in me, and humans can't understand how I'm so short compared to them. I stand out everywhere I go, and since I was old enough to take an interest in girls, they've been laughing at me." He took my hands in his, squeezing them gently. "You can trust me, Holly, I promise. I wasn't trying to hurt you or cause problems. After finally finding someone willing to go out with me, I was too afraid of your rejection, and the thought of it nearly sent me to my knees."

He placed a tender kiss on the back of each of my hands before letting them go and taking a step back. I didn't know what to say. Yes, I was sure his life had been as hard as he described, but the lack of trust hurt. Not every elf disliked half human elves. In fact, every elf at the North Pole didn't see a problem with it.

"Is there anything else you're neglecting to tell me? If so, now is the time to tell me." He shook his head. "Good. Now, I need to keep making my rounds and make sure we're on target for the next orders. You know how to reach me if you need something."

I reached for the door handle, but a hand closed around my shoulder before I could open it. "Holly, are we okay?"

"I don't know," I responded, opening the door and leaving before he could convince me otherwise.

Chapter 21

Noel stood outside the elevator when the doors opened a few floors from my destination. She took one look at me and dropped the bags in her hands with orders for the two elves with her to take care of them. She stepped inside and pressed the door close button and waited for them to shut before speaking.

"Holly, are you okay? What happened?"

I shook my head, the tears I'd been suppressing since running from Merric's office flowing down my cheeks. Noel pulled me into her arms, rubbing my back as she murmured softly in my ear. The doors opened again, but she didn't release me, and no one entered. Either we'd made my destination and no one waited, or they'd known better than to join us. I could be embarrassed about it later, but for now I was too heart-broken to care.

"Honey, what's wrong?" Noel asked, stepping back and wiping the tears from my cheeks while I sniffled. A hiccup echoed through the tiny room, and a few more tears leaked from my eyes.

"I think, I think I may have just broken up with Merric."

Instead of asking me what happened, she slammed her thumb against the first floor button and turned back to me. "This requires two things: hot chocolate and shopping. Wipe away those tears, dearie. We're having a girl's day the rest of today."

"But I have work to do." I sniffled again, and she produced a tissue from her pocket. She laughed when I arched an eyebrow. "I don't go anywhere without at least one. You never know when you'll need it. Now, work can wait. Everyone has it under control, and Merric will still be in the building. Let him do the heavy lifting. We're having some fun."

I didn't argue after that, but followed her from the building. Instead of following the same track as last time, Noel turned in the opposite direction. She seemed to know where she was heading, so I let her lead. It was several minutes before she spoke up, and I hoped I wouldn't break down and bawl like a baby again.

"So, what has you saying you think you broke up with him instead of that you actually did?"

My shoulders fell. "He asked if we were okay, and I told him I didn't know."

"Okay, first off, that's not a break up. It's more like an 'it's complicated' move. And second, what did he do to cause that?"

I waited until the human crowd around us thinned enough so that I wouldn't be overheard. "I confirmed with him that he's half human. He didn't even bother to tell me. I had to hear it through rumors and talk to his aunt before he'd tell me, and only after I asked him about it."

She dodged someone too busy on their phone to notice her and laughed when that same person walked into a light pole. "I don't blame you for being upset, but I'm sure he had his reasons for not saying anything."

"He did, and if I think about it, I understand them, but I'm too hurt he didn't trust me to bother trying to understand his side."

"And I don't blame you. Ooo, this looks like a nice place. Let's try this one." She led me inside another store, and for the next few hours we hopped from store to store, buying whatever fit her themes, or I liked for my office.

Dusk was setting before Noel, her team, and I made it back to the bakery. We stuffed our finds into one of the spare rooms on the main floor since her "office" was too full for any more decorations. Maybe Merric had a point and we were going a little crazy, but I was used to Christmas everywhere, and it would help keep the Christmas spirit all year.

When I mentioned checking in with Jewel on the status of our orders, Noel grabbed me by the shoulders and steered me to the elevator. "Holly, it's been a long day. You can check in with her tomorrow. Nothing you do tonight can change the amount of cookies and cakes baked today. You have a lot on your mind. I know you don't need me to tell you what to do, but if I were you, I'd make myself about three mugs of hot cocoa, soak in a hot bath, and find the nearest pair of fuzzy pajamas to crawl into with Christmas music playing in the background."

The elevator doors opened, and she shoved me inside. After spending more time with her, I'd grown used to the way she manhandled me when she wanted something. Or when she was excited to show off a new decoration.

"Yeah, that all sounds wonderful." It did, but I was still too upset by what happened earlier today with Merric to be overjoyed by the idea of relaxation. All I wanted to do was crawl into bed, worry, and hope he'd speak to me tomorrow.

"Can I give you my two cents worth on the situation?" Noel asked when we stepped inside and the doors closed behind us. When I nodded, she continued. "Do you still like Merric, even after he didn't tell you about his dad?"

There was no doubt in my mind about that. "Yes."

"And does knowing he's half human make a difference in how you feel about him?"

"No."

She set her hands on my shoulders and stared me dead in the eyes. "Do you think you can forgive him for not telling you?"

Absolutely. "Yes."

"Then forgive him. If you decide to stay with him, then more problems than this, bigger problems, will come at you. You can't just decide to throw in the towel whenever he hurts you or disappoints you. Life is going to throw you some curve balls, and you need to work them out, and you do that by talking, not running. Okay?"

I nodded, unable to speak. She was right. If I wanted to stay with Merric, I needed to talk this over with him. He hadn't set out to hurt me. Instead, he'd hoped to save himself some hurt. And though I was hurt by what happened, I still cared for him more than I'd cared for anyone else, even Jolly.

The elevator doors opened on my floor, and Noel and I stepped off and made our way to my apartment. The multicolored lights in the conference room glittered and sparkled as we passed, causing my heart to tighten. Noel noticed the direction of my gaze and squeezed my hand.

"It's okay. You'll jump this hurdle. I'm sure he understands."

Opening my apartment door, I stepped inside and stopped as my jaw hit the floor. Someone had redecorated my apartment, and I didn't need three guesses to know who had done it. In fact, I didn't need to even guess at who had set up the evergreen tree in the far corner of the room, fully decorated, or who had strung lights around the ceiling of every room I could see from the door, or draped garland from the cathedral ceiling in wavy patterns that crossed the room. Nope, I didn't need to guess. He'd even left the TV playing with a burning log fire on the screen.

A pizza box with an envelope laying on top of it sat on the coffee table in front of the first couch. Leaving Noel at the door, I sat on the couch and reached for the envelope. With shaking hands, I opened it to reveal a gorgeous Christmas Card. On the inside left side, which was strategically blank, was a note written in Merric's handwriting.

"Holly, you were right. I should have trusted you and told you the truth. From the moment I met you, I knew you were different. If Chip hadn't shunned me for who I am, and your mother remained friends with mine after she married my dad, then I should have known you would accept me. Please accept this offering as a further apology. I want to give us a second chance at this, if you'll let me. Since I wasn't sure if you were ready to see me yet, I thought I'd leave this card and peace offering for you instead of tracking you down. When you are ready, I'd love to see you. – Merric"

Setting the card back on the pizza box, I stood and toured my apartment as if seeing it again for the first time. Ornaments hung from the garland in the kitchen, reflecting off the light. Several Christmas cookie jars of varying styles lined the counter and Christmas magnets covered the fridge.

Even my bedroom was decorated. Lights glittered across my headboard and the dresser. Ornaments lay piled in fancy dishes around the room and a glittered star hung from the ceiling to light the room. When my tour was done, I rejoined Noel in the living room.

"I love that man," I laughed, covering my nose and mouth with my hands, still in shock. It was even more shocking when I realized that I did indeed love him. There were so many experiences that lay ahead, and I wanted no one else at my side for them except him. Today had been lonely, even with Noel and her team with me. I would notice something and want to share it with him, but he wasn't there. I'd done that, and now I needed to fix it.

"Yeah, I think he feels the same way," Noel murmured while I snatched up the pizza box. "You sharing that?"

"Not with you." She pouted, but I didn't let it distract me. "Do you know where Merric lives in the other building?"

Her eyes strayed between me and the pizza box several times before a bright smile lit her face. "Of course. He's on the top floor. The door on the left when you leave the elevator."

"Thanks. Are you going home now?"

She shrugged, following me to the door. "If you aren't sharing pizza, then I'm heading out for something to eat, but I'll join you on the way out."

"Sorry, Noel, but this pizza is important. If you want something to eat, I have some muffins here that me and Merric baked after our date. You could have a couple." Which was about all that was left after Merric had dug in the other day.

"Where?"

After Noel had inhaled her first muffin and grabbed two for the road, we left my apartment and took the elevator downstairs. More than one head turned with the scent of the pepperoni, ham, and cheese wafting through the air.

Since I hadn't been on a tour of the second building yet, Noel led the way inside. She showed me the commons area on the first level with its kitchen, dining area, and game room. The elevator was on the wall closest to my building, and she rode with me to her floor, which was about halfway up the building, and bid me goodnight. Then I finished the ride to the top floor, my nerves and stomach in knots.

The hall before me was empty when I exited the elevator, and no sounds resonated out of either apartment when I stood in front of Merric's door. At least I hoped it was his door. Now that I was standing here, I couldn't remember if Noel had told me that it was to the right or left. My hand hung suspended in the air as I considered finding someone to confirm which apartment was his. The last thing I wanted was to knock on the wrong door. It had been a bad enough day as it was.

I decided to take that course of action, but not before the door in front of me swung open, and Merric almost knocked me over in his rush to leave, and I squeaked. He bumped the pizza box out of my hands, and we both dove to catch it. He was faster than me, catching the box with ease. However, I doubted the contents would be the same after the box's tumble.

That didn't matter anymore when Merric stood and smiled down at me. It was a sad smile, and I couldn't tell what he was thinking, so I shrugged.

"If I eat an entire pizza by myself, then I deserve to spend the rest of my life alone. Plus, it's best fresh, and I don't know of anyone else I'd rather share food with but you, Merric." Unshed tears blurred my vision and I smiled at him when he flashed me his boyish grin.

The pizza box dropped to the floor, forgotten as Merric wrapped me in a tight hug and placed a kiss to the top of my head. When that didn't satisfy him, he tilted my head up and claimed my lips. It was the best apology I'd ever been given. All of the hurt and fear we'd experienced today melted away, replaced by our new trust and the love that blossomed between us.

"So, no pizza?" I asked when we broke the kiss and he rested his forehead against mine.

"Yes, pizza. It may look a bit rough, but it tastes the same going down. I take it you saw your apartment."

I laughed and stole another kiss before retrieving the discarded box. He led me into his apartment. It was neat, tidy, and everything had its place. Knowing him as I did, I wasn't surprised by this. While he took the box from me and moved toward the kitchen, I gave myself a self guided tour. It was a nice sized apartment, but much smaller than mine. A few Christmas decorations sat around on shelves or hung from hooks, but otherwise there were few decorations of any kind.

"Here you go." Merric found me in the living room and handed me a plate with three slices of pizza. "Want to sit and talk as we eat or watch a movie?"

"I think we need to talk."

He nodded and motioned for me to take a seat on his couch. While I sat on one end, he took the other. Instead of talking right away, I stuffed my face with pizza. It had been a while since I'd last eaten, and if I was going to have a deep conversation, then I wanted to do it with my belly full. Merric didn't push me, but ate his pizza right along with me. When we finished, he took my plate to the kitchen and returned with a glass of ice cold milk for both of us.

"I'm not into eating as many sweets as most elves," he explained while he sat back in his seat. "I prefer well balanced meals, unlike your diet which is almost entirely sugar. My dad wanted me to attend human schools because I'm half human, and yes, he knows Mom is an elf. He's known since before they were married, and he loves her because that's part of who she is. I know you said that knowing that I'm half human doesn't bother or upset you, but I wanted to be sure. Does it?"

His gaze pleaded for the truth. Reaching between us, I rested my hand against his cheek. He closed his eyes and leaned into my touch and my stomach flipped. He was so vulnerable.

"Merric, I love you."

Chapter 22

Those weren't the words I'd meant to come out of my mouth, but they were the ones on repeat over and over in my brain, so it made sense. Still, my jaw clamped shut at my admission, and Merric's eyes popped open and rounded to the size of saucers. In that moment, panic struck and my heart stuttered. Yes, he obviously liked me, but did he love me in return?

His eyes softened and he cupped my face in his hands, twining his fingers into my hair. "You know what I like best about you?"

With his hands holding my head, I couldn't shake it. "No."

"At first it was your smile. Then it was your cookie scent. Now it's the way your eyes brighten whenever you see me. I hope I never do anything that makes that go away, or that causes the hurt I saw in them today. I love you too, Holly. I always will, I promise you that."

Instead of kissing me as I expected, Merric pulled me into his arms and held me, swaying side to side while rubbing a circle on my back. Content to stay in his arms, I wrapped mine around him and soaked in his warmth. He kissed the top of my head, but continued to hold me. This was the best moment of my day.

"Thank you for decorating my apartment. I love it." My whispered words were muffled by his white shirt, but he heard them and chuckled.

"I hoped you'd like it, at least enough to forgive me. The pizza was for just in case that wasn't enough."

"It helped."

Continuing to laugh, Merric ran a thumb over my cheek. "Well, now you know, and I can relax." He narrowed his eyes at my grimace.

"We need to tell everyone. Be as honest with them as you should have been with me."

He paled, shaking his head ever so slightly. "No, Holly. You don't understand the consequences of that."

"I don't think you understand how many elves here don't mind if you're half human."

"But it's not those elves that worry me. It's the ones who will take an issue with it that will cause us problems."

I placed my hands on either side of his face to stop him from shaking his head. It also allowed him to focus on me, and my voice hardened. "Then I don't want them here. We're a team, and we're going to remain that way. Anyone who doesn't want to be on the team doesn't have to be here."

"The Grand Opening is in four days, Holly. Santa will be here. We can't do this right now."

"And we can't wait either. Be honest with them and with yourself. Do not hide from who you are. Accept it and embrace it. Once you do, no ornery elf will be able to stop you, but staying as you are only hinders you. Be proud of who you are, Merric, because I'm proud of you."

Tears glistened in his eyes, pooling until he blinked and they spilled over to trail down his cheeks. "I'm so happy I met you. From the moment I saw your picture I knew you were the one. I must have done something right in order to receive you as this year's Christmas present."

Then he kissed me. And it was wonderful. And somehow I ended up pulled onto his lap. I'd been too wrapped up in his kiss to notice.

"There's no changing your mind is there," he moaned when I broke off the kiss. "We have to tell the other elves."

"Face it, they already know, but they're waiting for confirmation. Can you have everyone meet on the main floor first thing in the morning? I want to tell them before they begin working and get it over with. If they have a problem, they can either leave or speak with us directly." I set my head on his shoulder and snuggled close to him while his arms tightened around me. If I never had to leave the warmth of his embrace, it would be too soon.

We stayed like that for what could have been hours. Merric leaned back into the couch and I stayed curled against him while he played with my hair. Little by little my muscles relaxed into goo and the only thoughts filling my head were of Merric. I refused to worry about tomorrow, content to stay in his arms knowing he loved me back.

"I should walk you home," he murmured, waking me from a light sleep. I'd been drifting in and out of sleep, and by the husky tone of his voice, he'd been having the same fight. Though his words said to move, neither of us did. Even his hands in my hair had stilled.

"Is your couch comfortable?"

He chuckled and slowly sat up. "I'm sure it is, but your father would kill me if I let you stay here. Not to mention our mothers. I prefer to live a long, healthy life, thank you very much."

We managed to stand up without falling over, and he led me from the apartment. When I told him I could walk back myself, he scolded me and warned me about going outside alone at night, even if I was only going between buildings. That was new to me since I'd never had to worry about going outside at night back in Christmas Village, but I heeded his warning. He wouldn't have given it if he didn't feel it was necessary. In fact, he didn't leave my side until we stood in front of my apartment.

His normally spiky hair was in disarray and his white shirt was wrinkled. I was certain I didn't look any better, but from the expression he wore, no one would be able to tell. No doubt if I had bed head he'd still stare at me like I was an angel.

"Good night, my love." He kissed my hands, my cheeks, my nose, and my lips before turning around and walking back down the hall.

I shut myself into my apartment, a perma-smile frozen on my face. I was in love, and I didn't care who knew it. All I wanted to do was call Jolly, but Papa would kill me for calling this late. Instead, I settled for climbing into bed and shooting off an email to my sister telling her I had news and to call me when she was available. My phone vibrated right after I'd turned the tablet's screen off, and I checked my phone to find a message from Merric that he'd made it back to his room safely and that he missed me already. I sent back that I couldn't wait to see him in the morning and I missed him too. Now that our feelings were out in the open, it was much easier to be open with him.

. . .

Voices carried around the room, echoing off the walls and amplifying to the point where I wanted to ask Santa for ear plugs this Christmas. Every available space held an elf, and Merric stood beside me at the front of the horde. The excitement from last night seemed to have worn off for him and he fidgeted side to side as nerves raced through him. Even when I held his hand, he still twitched, his eyes roaming the crowd. It didn't help that Carol stood directly in front of our tiny platform, which had been set up so everyone could see us as well as hear us.

"You ready?" I asked him, squeezing his hand as I spoke. He shrugged. Obviously not ready, but like me, wanted to have this over with and move on with the day. "Would you mind getting their attention again?"

"If I don't puke first," he muttered under his breath but whistled to gain their attention. The sharpness of the sound cut off all conversation, and left my ear closest to him with a slight ring.

I cleared my throat in the sudden silence and stared out over the gathered crowd. "Hello, everyone. You're probably wondering why we've called you all here. Well, Merric and I have talked and there's something we want you to know.

"Over the last few days, rumors have been spread and others have asked me about my relationship with Merric. Yes, we are a couple." I took a deep breath. "And yes, I know he is half human."

Rumbled conversations exploded in the silence. No one outright yelled, but from many faces, they weren't happy about the news. However, just as many smiled back at us. One older elf even told two younger girls to "Cool it." I let them grumble and get it out of their systems before bringing their attention back to me. Some still scowled, but others appeared pacified.

"For some of you, that news is a shock. Others of you have assumed this was the case. However, it doesn't change anything. Merric is still my assistant, and always will be for however long he wants the position. My father and Santa gave him the job, and I guarantee they know about his heritage. They trust him to do the job, a job which he has earned with his elf nature and human knowledge. I know I couldn't run this bakery without his help.

"Now, we are a team, and teams stick together and are unified. I hope you all will give Merric a chance and truly get to know him, but if you refuse, that's all right. You're still welcome to work with us. If that is not an option for you, leave your name with Liz at the front desk and pack your bags. This job is about spreading love and Christmas cheer. You can't do that while hate, distrust, and ignorance are buried in your heart. After all, Christmas is for everyone.

"Thank you all for listening. If you plan to stay, please head up to your floors. Merric and I will visit each floor, and if you have questions or concerns, we will address them then. For those who do not wish to stay, leave your name and your position so that we know what positions we have to fill. Okay, this meeting is adjourned."

At first there was little movement. Then everyone moved. Thankfully all the elves controlled themselves so we didn't have chaos ensue during the main floor exodus. Like the day of the hot chocolate fiasco, some took the stares while others the elevator…and others approached the front desk, wrote their names down, and walked out the front door. There were more of those than I'd expected, but less than I had feared. However, when Liz brought the list over to me when the room had cleared, I found a huge problem. Most of those who'd left were bakers.

"Well, that's nearly a quarter of our baking staff," Merric murmured as he read over my shoulder. "I was expecting more, so this isn't too bad, but it'll still put us behind. Any thoughts?"

I gave a sharp nod. "Yup. Make our rounds to each floor quick and then call a meeting with the Head Bakers. I have a plan that may not work, but it's something."

"All right. Let's head up. And Holly," he took my hand and stopped me when we reached the stairs. "Thank you. You were right. I needed to be honest, not only with them, but with myself. It's kind of liberating."

"Next time I'll let you handle the speech then."

Merric snorted a laugh and led the way up the stairs. "No, thank you. I'll pass on that. Your speech was better than anything I could have come up with on the spot. Let's do this."

It didn't take long to make our rounds up the building. No one really had any concerns. Those who had stayed were willing to accept Merric, and that was that.

At each floor, we asked the Head Baker to meet us upstairs. When we joined them in the conference room, their chatter stopped. Of all those who had left, not one of them had been a Head Baker. We were extremely blessed for that. At least one person on each floor knew how to bake.

"Okay, well as you've probably heard, we lost a significant number of bakers today. That's going to put a strain on us to keep up the delivery schedule we've been given, but until we can hire more bakers, I have an idea. It's only a Band Aid for the problem, but I think we can do it."

Lewis, the pumpkin and pecan pie Head Baker, raised his hand, speaking at the same time. "Before we begin discussing a plan, I want to say something. I had my assumptions about Merric from the moment I met him, and it never once bothered me. I came here to do a job, and that's what I'm going to do. Everyone in this room had better feel the same way. If not, there's the door."

Every eye in the room glanced around, and more than one person took a long, hard look at Carol. She grunted, smacking her hand on the table. "Don't look at me, you elves. I knew what he was coming into this. If I'd had a problem with him, I would have turned right around and headed right back down that elevator. I'm here to bake, not cause more problems for my nephew."

"Then that settles that," Merric announced, and pulled the only empty chair out so I could sit. "All right, Holly, explain your plan."

It didn't take me long to explain that my plan was to focus on each individual order one at a time. If a cookie, muffin, or cake wasn't on the order, the elves baking that product would assist the other levels that had the most quantities being produced. It would require more communication and better organization, but it could be done, for a short period of time, anyway.

"I don't know if some of my bakers are up to it," Lewis stated, running a hand over his hair. "Some of their pies still come out goopy. And let's not even mention the pie having a golden crust."

"Maybe a cookie or cake would better suite them anyway," Carol interjected. "If we put the word out soon that we need more bakers, maybe we can fill the vacant positions within a few weeks and we won't have to worry about doing this long."

"That's the hope," I told them. "It may not even work, but we have to try. We don't have much of a choice. We can't lose any accounts, and Santa is counting on us. Christmas spirit is already at an all time low. We have to do our part."

"What about baking in shifts?" Cherry suggested. "Or making longer hours?"

"They can't bake without a Head Baker present," I warned. "Back home it wouldn't be a problem, but we have too many unseasoned bakers. Would you all be willing to do shifts or longer hours?"

Carol shook her head. "Let's try your plan first. If it doesn't work, we'll go back to the drawing board. Merric, what's the next order look like?"

For the next half an hour we reorganized our team to the best fit for the products we needed. Hope blossomed inside my chest once again. We could do this, and even if we failed, we'd tried and given it our best shot. Even Santa couldn't fault us for that.

"Which floor do you want me and Merric on?" I asked the bakers before they stood to leave. They each wore surprised expressions, but no one spoke. "We need everyone to help. I'm done going from floor to floor. I trust you all to handle your people, especially when some of you are doubled up. Now, I can bake, and Merric will help me. He can at least read ingredients and measure them. Where do you want us?"

"Pumpkin muffins," Merric murmured from above me, gaining all of our attention. "You said this order and the next want a specialty item. We make pumpkin muffins."

"Nope." I grinned. "They want a specialty cookie. I've got one we can make. It's an old family recipe. Never mind. Merric and I are taking half of the room on the top baking level. We'll need the ovens overnight."

Merric quirked an eyebrow at me and I laughed. Everyone stood and left to gather their people. Once they had all left, I sprinted to my office and grabbed the book Papa had given me. Inside were all of our family recipes from generations past and the one cookie recipe that could make this Christmas baking special. It was the first cookie Mama and Papa had baked together, and Papa's parents before that. Now, I wanted to bake it with Merric.

"You ready to go?" I asked before reaching the conference room. Merric was already stepping out the door, his phone in his hand. He was mid-dial, but stopped.

"I will be, but first, I need to let Chip know what happened."

"He's going to kill me." Closing my eyes, I wanted to bang my head against a wall. No way did I want to be present for that conversation.

"No, actually, I think he'll be quite proud of you. I know I am." When I opened my eyes, he winked at me and I blushed. "Then I need to change. There is no way I want to spill food on my clothes."

"Hurry up, buddy. Time's a wastin'!"

Without another word, we raced to the elevator.

Chapter 23

Merric met me on the top floor of the operational baking levels. We were paired with the fruit cake baking elves, but they ignored us in their rush to mass produce as many cakes as they could manage. There was little chatter, and Christmas songs played from the far side of the room. Everyone was focused and ready to bake…except my baking companion.

His strut across the room slowed to a stop when he saw me leaning on the countertop, hovering over the cookbook. With a smirk, he eyed me from head to toe and back up again. I refused to let myself blush, but stood straight and matched his pose by crossing my arms over my chest.

"You ready to bake, elf?" I asked him, giving him a seductive wink. Shaking his head with a grin and a laugh, he closed the distance between us. He wrapped his arms around me from behind and turned us so we could both see the recipe. Thankfully he was tall enough to read it over my shoulder.

"This doesn't look too complicated," he murmured into my hair.

His breath tickled my ear and I shivered. It still amazed me that we'd only known one another for a few weeks, but it was like we'd known one another our entire lives. He could make me laugh like no one else could, and being with him made my homesickness tolerable.

"It's more difficult than it appears." I leaned back into him and lifted my head to stare at him. "It's a touchy meringue cookie. One wrong move and you've messed it up, and we have several batches to make tonight. Every oven on our side of the room will be filled."

He did a quick scan of the ovens I mentioned, and I could see him counting. "Okay, that's it?"

"For today. Tomorrow we're doing it all over again. They have to stay in the oven overnight so they take time. If we don't have enough ovens on this level, we'll start using the ovens on the next floor. You ready to start?"

"If you're by my side to teach me, I'm always ready."

"Remember you said that in an hour."

The rest of the day went as planned. A few times we were interrupted to help with other cookies or to answer questions about the order. I never did ask Merric what Papa had to say about what I'd done, and he never mentioned it. By the end of the day, my feet hurt and we'd started filling the ovens on the next floor. My baking companion had caught on to the recipe's unique traits and quickly learned what it meant to "beat until stiff."

One by one the Head Bakers found us and gave a report of the day. We decided to meet a half an hour early before backing began the next day to determine who baked what and what was baked. It would be tedious to start every day like that, but it was necessary until we could hire more workers.

By the end of the day, my feet were killing me. Merric was visibly worn out, and I wasn't much better. He'd never done a bake-a-thon day before, and my late night and lack of sleep was catching up to me.

"I'm sorry, Merric, but I think we're going to have to put off the tour of the city until after this mess is figured out," I whined, drying my hands as we finished cleaning up.

He was sitting on the ground with his back against a cupboard, his long legs extended in front of him. When I'd mentioned making one last batch of cookies after we'd washed all of our dishes, he'd rebelled. Then he'd rolled his eyes when I'd laughed and told him I was joking, but he hadn't stood back up.

"Don't apologize. We have a responsibility to do our jobs first and foremost. Plus, it's not like the city is going to pick itself up and walk away. It'll be there when the new year rolls around and the orders slow down."

Sliding down to join him on the floor, I intertwined our arms and took his hand in mine. "I'm tired, but I want to spend more time with you. Want to watch a movie in my apartment?"

"As long as I can order pizza and you have muffins available for dessert."

"I won't say no to the pizza, and I just may have a few muffins left, but you have to share them with me."

He gave me a quick peck on the lips before rolling to a stand and helping me to my feet. "I promise you'll get at least one. After that, I make no promises. Let me call in dinner while we head up. Just no chick-flicks, okay?"

"Really? We're watching Rudolph. I found a copy stuffed in my suitcase. Jolly must have done it. She knows it's my favorite."

"I see. Well then who am I to mess with your movie plans?"

"Exactly."

By the time we reached the apartment, the pizza was ordered. Merric decided not to wait until the pizza arrived and dug into the muffins. He did do as he promised and saved me one. In fact, I had two. The second I stole and hid while he was in the bathroom. When he returned, he grumbled and searched for it until the pizza arrived.

With a full belly, I relaxed on the couch next to Merric's warm body. The combination had my already tired body and mind heading into a food coma. I didn't even make it to the Island of Misfit Toys.

When I woke up to my alarm blaring, I was sprawled out under the covers in my bed. And I still wore yesterday's clothes. My tired brain tried to make sense of how that was possible until I remembered I'd fallen asleep during the movie. Merric had to have carried me to bed when the movie ended.

Climbing from bed, I padded down the hall to the living room. He was gone, but a note lay on the kitchen island. As always, I recognized Merric's handwriting in seconds. His letter confirmed he'd put me to bed and he would see me at our meeting before work began. That jumpstarted my day, and I raced to clean up, taking extra time with my hair and makeup, even though it wouldn't survive an hour of baking.

I was closing the apartment door behind me when my eyes wandered to the view of the city outside and reality struck hard. We had two days until Santa showed up. Not only was the building not ready, but we were already having a difficult time filling orders and the season's rush hadn't even set in. Plus, I hadn't been able to send any cookies to Christmas Village yet. Stepping up to the glass, I leaned my forehead against it and closed my eyes, willing my heart to slow down.

Steady footsteps echoed up the hall and stopped when they rounded the corner. Since the Head Bakers weren't supposed to start arriving in the conference room for another ten minutes, it could only be Merric coming to check on me. Today he would need to be the strong one. I'd spent my strength being strong yesterday when I announced Merric's heritage and excused too many bakers from service.

"What if this doesn't work?" I asked him, keeping my eyes closed and hoping my voice didn't quiver. "What if we can't succeed?"

"In my opinion, you already have." The voice was male, deep, and not Merric, but equally as recognizable.

"Papa!"

Standing straight, I took one look at him and bolted down the hall toward him. He caught me in his arms and twirled me around like I was a kid again. A strangled laugh escaped me before unexpected sobs tore through my body. There went all the time I'd taken to look pretty, thrown right out the window. But it didn't matter. Papa was here, and now everything would be okay, except...

My tears stopped as panic stole my breath and I pushed away from him. "Santa isn't here, is he?"

Papa chuckled as he shook his head. Relief swamped me and I almost sagged to the floor. My body and emotions couldn't keep taking these ups and downs like this. Maybe I needed more sleep...or a cup of hot chocolate since I'd skipped eating breakfast.

"Then why are you here?" I loved that he was here, but I wasn't sure if it was a good or bad sign yet.

Another set of footsteps echoed up the hall, stopping at the conference room. With a moment's hesitation, they followed Papa's lead and came toward my hall. This time it had to be Merric, and I breathed a sigh of relief when he turned the corner and stopped dead in his tracks. His eyes found mine before swinging to Papa.

"Chip, what are you doing here?"

Papa wrapped his arm around my shoulders. "I heard you were

understaffed, and since we have no bakery in Christmas Village, some of the elves were growing bored. A little too bored. So, I brought them down here to help you out. I hope you don't mind, but I couldn't rein them in once they set foot in the bakery. They've started baking. Some of your elves have joined them already. We won't step on your toes. Just tell us where to go and we'll be there."

"Thank you so much, Papa." I wrapped my arms around him, giving him a gentle squeeze. When I released him, Merric stepped forward to shake Papa's hand. I watched the two of them, still in shock that Papa was here, and that he'd brought help.

"Why are we still standing here?" Papa laughed, pushing us ahead of him. "Let's get moving. There's baking to do!"

We hadn't even rounded the corner to the conference room when Merric reached out and took my hand. He smiled at me when I looked up at him, and I returned it. Already Merric was staking his claim in front of Papa, but by the twinkle in my father's eyes when I peeked at him from the corner of my eye, he didn't mind one bit. That was a blessed relief. Now I had to survive Mama and Jolly's questions when they arrived in a few short days. Was it too late to plan a vacation?

The elevator ride to the second floor was quiet, but when I stepped out of it, someone screamed my name and barreled into me, knocking both of us to the floor. My backside hit the tile hard, but the pain was pushed to the back of my mind when I recognized the elf who'd tackled me. What was she doing here?

"Jolly!"

I hugged my sister in a bear hug that mimicked the clamped embrace she gave me in return. When neither of us could breathe, we eased our holds, but didn't let go, or stand up. Until this moment I hadn't realized how much I'd missed her. There had been so much happening that had occupied my mind. Now she was here, and I couldn't let her go.

"I'm so happy to see you." I squeezed her tighter, afraid she would disappear into thin air if I let her go. "I can't believe you're here."

"Tell me about it. I was under the impression it would be years before I visited you. Now help me up."

Sitting up, I narrowed my eyes at her and she plastered a smile of angelic innocence on her face. "Help you up? Silly, you're the reason we're on the floor."

"It's not my fault you have awful balance," she whined. Any other time and that comment would have forced me to my feet in irritation, and then I'd have to help her up, but not today. Nope, I crossed my arms and glared. Even when she pouted, I didn't move. The standoff had begun, and I wasn't about to lose. Not this time.

"Ladies, why don't you let me help you?" Merric's voice broke into our glaring contest, and Jolly's eyes widened before a sly grin snaked across her lips. She'd been dying to meet the boy, and now she was here face to face with him. He'd either live to regret offering to help us, or he'd make a friend for life. I wasn't quite sure which was worse. At least it wasn't up to me to decide.

Reaching down, Merric took both of our hands and pulled us up from the floor. I took a few seconds to dust myself off, but Jolly skipped that step. She closed what little distance was between her and Merric to stare up into his face. Her eyes narrowed, but he never backed down or stepped away from her. In fact, he studied her back with the same intent stare-down that she was giving him.

After thirty seconds or more, I was sure I'd need to break them up, but Jolly nodded, took a step back, and stated, "He'll do."

Like she had a choice in the matter. It was at least comforting that she didn't hate him already, for whatever reason.

Clearing my throat, I gained her attention, as well as Merric's. "Don't tell me you're here to bake."

"Nope. I'm not here to bake."

She sounded a bit too happy about that. "Then what are you doing here? Moral support? Vacation?"

"Nope. My job."

"Yeah, you still haven't told me what that is yet…"

Her eyes lit up and she bounced up and down on the balls of her feet. "Yes, because I wanted to tell you in person, remember? Okay, so I didn't plan this, it just sort of started happening, and before I knew it I was offered the position."

"Which is?" I offered, arching my eyebrows in impatience.

"I'm Santa's personal assistant."

"Hold the eggnog, what?"

My sister, the craziest elf of all, was none other than Santa's personal assistant? What had happened while I was gone? First the bakery burned down, and now this? What else didn't I know about?

I opened my mouth to ask, but before any words could form, Papa tapped me on the shoulder. "I know you have lots to discuss with your sister, but right now we have some work to do."

He was right. There were still orders to be filled, and decorations to display. Taking a deep breath, I exhaled slowly, taking the time to think.

"Okay. Papa, I need a handful of your elves to work on specialty cookies. With your elves here, that will free up me and Merric."

Merric held his hand up, stopping me. "Actually, I'd like to do some baking today, with Chip's help. It shouldn't take long. I don't think it should, anyway."

So now I was going to be by myself running this show while Merric...baked? Who knew I'd created a monster? Nodding I peered at Jolly.

"If you aren't baking, what are you doing?"

"I'm prepping Santa's apartment. Apparently it's the apartment across the hall from Merric's in the other building. At least that's what I hear. I haven't been over there yet."

"It's the one on the right," I confirmed. "Merric's is on the left."

Jolly snickered. "You would know that. Okay, well I'm on my way to make sure it's all set for Santa to arrive. He'll arrive tomorrow night. Let's move people. We don't have time to waste!"

She snatched me into a quick hug before skipping toward the staircase to run down to the first floor. Merric kissed my cheek and led Papa up the stairs to the next level, leaving me standing alone. A few elves I knew from Christmas Village stood off to the side.

"Well, let's find you all a place to work, shall we?"

Chapter 24

The day ran smooth with little hiccups to overcome. Our lead inventory elf had been one of the elves who'd left, and it just so happened that Flakes, Papa's lead inventory elf, happened to come down South with him. She began training those left on the team in the best inventory practices known to human or elf. Soon I had a request to order more supplies, and it took me a while of sitting in my office to figure out how to send Merric the order I'd entered. When I finally finished, I hopped around my office in a giddy circle. That was where Noel and Jolly found me, and I stopped when I saw they'd caught me.

"You've gotten weirder since you left. I blame Merric," Jolly stated, her voice dry as dirt, but full of complete seriousness.

"Well, it wasn't me," Noel added with a giggle. "Okay, maybe a little was me."

"What do you two want in my office? And don't you know how to knock?"

"Since when do I have to knock?" Jolly strolled further into the room to walk around my desk and stare out my window. "This view is nice, but it's lacking a natural perspective. How can you stand to live cooped up like this?"

"You grow used to it, plus you should see it when it's dark and there are lights all over. It's beautiful in its own way."

She didn't look convinced, but I didn't care to explain further. It wasn't any skin off my nose if she didn't like New York. It was my home now, and I loved it.

"So, what are you two up to?"

"We need some help decorating Santa's apartment," Noel explained. "Would you like to help?"

I shook my head. "I'd love to, but I just finished this project, and I need to check with Jewel on the status of the orders going out. You two can decorate his apartment, but I need to be sure we're running like a well oiled machine before Santa arrives."

"When did you grow up?" Jolly asked, studying me. "It suits you."

"Thanks, Jol. Don't worry, you'll end up there someday soon too."

She grunted. "I hope not. Just because I'm Santa's personal assistant doesn't mean I'm growing up anytime soon. I like being my immature self, and it doesn't seem to bother him."

"For now," I muttered, then waved them from my office while I followed them out. When they stepped off the elevator on the main floor, I followed them out and headed right while they ventured left.

I found Jewel in her usual place on the opposite end of the first floor. She handed out orders and directed the traffic of the elves she managed with a finesse I hoped to have one day. For now, I settled for watching her work. When she noticed me, she waved and called that all was on schedule and we'd have the second and third orders complete by the end of the day, which included the cookies Merric and I had made yesterday.

Not wanting to bother her, I strolled up the stairs to the next floor, and for the rest of the day, I did as I usually did, going from one floor to the other. When I caught sight of Merric and Papa on the top baking floor, I started toward them, but they motioned me away. Since everyone had the baking under control, I meandered back to my office and settled for figuring out all of the new computer programs that would help smooth out our production.

That was where Papa found me later, staring at the computer screen hoping it would spit out the answers to the questions I was yelling at it. He chuckled and took a seat on the other side of my desk. It was still weird to be on this side of a desk in an office that was mine.

"I see you're getting the hang of technology," he laughed at me, and I scowled once more at the monitor before turning in my chair to give him my full attention.

"It reminds me I'm still learning this job." I bit my lip. "I made a judgment call in telling the elves who couldn't work with Merric to leave. I thought it was best then, and I still think that, but it's caused problems and it put us behind. Without your help, and the help of the elves you brought with you, we'd never survive, and the season is only beginning." He nodded, but remained quiet, so I plugged away. "If you'd been in my shoes, what would you have done? How would you have made the situation work?"

He shook his head and leaned forward, resting his elbows on his knees. "Holly, stop beating yourself up. I can't know for sure what I would have done, but I would hope that if I was ever in that situation that I'd have the guts to do what you and Merric did. You stood up for what you know is right and you plunged into it head first. That's why we're here. You know as well as I do that you can't make a true Christmas cookie without love."

"A cookie without love is just a cookie." I repeated Papa's saying, smiling at him and he nodded.

"That's correct. I'm proud of you, as is your mother, Santa, and Mrs. Claus. You've grown up so much. Now, I'm going to make myself comfortable in one of your guest rooms. Jolly wants to stay in your room, but I told her that was up to you. I'm not sure she listened to me, so you may find her suitcase on your bed."

That silly girl. Shaking my head, I stood and walked with Papa toward the apartment. The scent of pizza greeted us, and the closer we drew to my apartment, the stronger the smell. Merric deserved the best Christmas gift of all time for introducing me to pizza.

"Papa, how did you all make it here? You didn't bring a herd of dragons, did you?"

"Of course not. Santa had Jolly charter a bus for us somewhere north of here and we rode the bus to the city and it dropped us off outside your building. When we leave, we'll go back the same way. It makes us less conspicuous."

I'll say. Someone would have seen them arrive if they'd brought dragons and sleighs. My questions died on my lips when we entered my living room to find boxes of pizza on the table with mugs of hot cocoa surrounding them. Noel and Jolly sat on the couch and Merric stood by the window. His eyes sought mine, and he grinned and held up a plate for me.

"What's this?" I asked him, taking the plate and staring down at the cookies.

"Holly for my Holly," he laughed as I examined his creation. Sugar cookies in the shape of holly leaves with green frosting covering them were placed together so they formed a small, oddly shapen box that was also held together by frosting. Red cinnamon candies decorated the cookies as holly berries.

"Go ahead. Open it," Merric laughed when all I did was stare at the box.

"This is amazing," I told him, lifting the lid. Inside was a small, thin jewelry box. My first thought was a ring, and my heart had skipped a beat, but a second thought calmed my racing heart. It was too thin to be a ring. Handing the plate back to Merric to hold, I took the jewelry box out of the cookie box and opened it. "Merric!"

Inside the box were two large, holly earrings. Emerald leaves were accented by ruby berries in a gold gilded setting. They were as impressive as the ruby jewelry he'd given to me on our first date.

"They're for you to wear tomorrow. For good luck." He leaned in and kissed my cheek, which caused our female audience to mock swoon and giggle. Ignoring them, I planted a kiss on Merric's lips. If my father hadn't been present, I may have deepened the kiss to tease the girls, but I wouldn't dare in front of him. It would be... awkward.

"Thank you," I whispered, meeting his eyes before giving him another peck on the lips. "I love them."

"I hope so, and I hope it's not too cliché to give you holly cookies and jewelry."

Shaking my head, I set my attention on the pizza. "Nope, it's not. I think when most people back home associate my name with anything, it's 'Holly Jolly Christmas'. It's different here." I looked to Jolly and shrugged. "No offense, but I like being my own person now."

She mimicked my shrug. "Oh I understand. Now that you're gone, I don't know if I could go back to sharing the limelight."

Leave it to Jolly.

"Okay, let's dig in. I'm starving."

IT WASN'T my alarm that woke me, but Jolly's arm swatting me in the face as she slept. After pushing her away from me, and somehow she slept through it, I checked the time. There was just over a half an hour until my alarm went off. Groaning, I cursed Jolly for her stubborn persistence in convincing me to let her sleep in my room. Once my brain remembered that Santa arrived tonight, the fog of sleep that threatened to pull me back under evaporated.

Knowing I'd never fall back to sleep, I crawled from bed and readied for the day. Jolly hadn't moved except to roll onto my side of the bed. My irritation slipped a little as I watched her sleep, knowing our time together was short. Before I left the bedroom, I kissed her forehead and tucked the covers in around her like Mama always did with us. Then I went in search of cold pizza and hot chocolate, the new breakfast of champions.

Papa still snored away as I passed his room, and the apartment was still when I snuck out after eating. To be honest, it was too early for elf nor beast to be awake. However, my gut told me that Merric would be awake, so I sent him a text telling him good morning. He responded seconds later with a smiley face and an invitation to meet him in his office when I was ready to start my day. It didn't surprise me that on such a big day as this that he would already be hard at work.

When I knocked on his office door frame minutes later, his head shot up from staring at the tablet on his desk. "Well, that was quick," he laughed, coming around the desk to plant a kiss on my lips and pull me into a warm embrace. "Couldn't sleep either?"

"Jolly tried to give me a black eye in her sleep."

He chuckled and led me to my normal seat, and instead of going back to his, he sat in the chair beside mine after shifting it so he could look at me. "So, Santa arrives tonight and the big day is tomorrow. How do you feel about this?"

"Nervous. Scared. Excited. You name it, I feel it. What do you feel?"

"Confident."

I arched an eyebrow at him. "Explain."

"Holly, we've done everything we could to make this work with such short notice. Santa and Chip couldn't have asked for much more than what we've given. They're not going to come in here condemning our shortcomings after all we've done to make this succeed. So you see, I'm confident. We made mistakes but we've learned, and that's all that's required."

"We could have done better."

"And we could have done worse. Come on. I think we need to start our day off right. Let's start the hot chocolate machines so that they're ready when the elves arrive, and let's greet everyone at the door and wish them a wonderful day."

His energy caused me to giggle. It was infectious. "You want to do that? Really? You?"

His cheeks brightened to a pretty pink. "They need as much encouragement as we do that we're all doing a good job, so we need to be the ones to tell them. We aren't the only nervous ones, I can guarantee it."

"Truer words have never been spoken. Let's go."

The first elves were entering the building for the day when we exited the elevator after setting up each hot chocolate station. They all grinned or laughed at Merric's enthusiastic greeting, and a few even gave us both a hug before heading to their respective floors. We continued to greet everyone until the last of the elves trailed in. Not one of them turned down Merric's greeting or showed any kind of distain. It encouraged me as much as it did him.

"Well, I'll check our incoming orders and you do your thing," he sighed. "Oh, and I have to purchase that order you sent me. We can't run out of supplies now."

"Nope, that would look bad. Merric, do you think it would be okay if I started pulling elves aside for quick personal one on one interviews? Just to be sure they're happy with their position and to hear any concerns? Or would you like to be there? Or is it a stupid idea?"

He chuckled at my rapid fire questions and placed a kiss on the top of my head. "Go for it. It can't hurt."

The rest of the day I spent in interviews with the elves we'd first hired. Papa joined me for some of the interviews once he'd heard what I was up to. He asked questions I hadn't thought about, and nodded when I asked follow-up questions to various answers. When quitting time came, everyone made sure their stations and floors were spotless. We wanted to make sure Santa's first impression was perfect. Noel left the music playing on each floor to keep the Christmas mood, as well as leaving on any Christmas lights. All other lights were turned off so the multicolored glow could greet whoever entered the room.

"You're going to wear a whole in the floor," Merric warned me after I'd been pacing my apartment living room for over an hour trying to rid myself of nervous energy. The sun had long since set, and we were expecting Santa any minute. "We'll be fine."

"I know, but this is it, Merric. This is the final moment. Can you think of anything we've missed?"

"If there is, it's too late now."

"What about a cookie tray?" Noel asked from where she lay on a couch. Papa sat on another sofa and Jolly sat curled on the opposite end. She kept checking her phone, which didn't settle my nerves any.

"Will you stop that?" I asked her, and the words had barely left my mouth before the phone chirped a notification.

She opened the message and grinned. "They're five minutes out. It's show time people."

Chapter 25

We made it to the roof with plenty of time to spare before a sleigh pulled by three dragons landed soundlessly. The lead dragon was huge, and I recognized him before they'd even landed. Of course Lunar would lead the team, and if he was here, that meant Vixen was the dragon on his right flank. The scowling dragon on Lunar's left could only be Ridge.

And the man stepping out of the sleigh was the one and only St. Nicholas, a.k.a. Santa Claus. We'd spoken on several occasions, but none like this. No one knew for sure if he was human or elf, but he was taller than Merric. Dressed in his usual red trousers, white shirt, and red suspenders, he looked the part of every child's fantasy. Well, he was a bit less rotund and more muscular. Mrs. Claus exited the sleigh after him in a dressy pants suit.

"Mama!" I cried, and ignoring our important guests, I ran to her and threw my arms around her neck when she followed Mrs. Claus out of the sleigh. She hugged me in return and kissed my cheek before pulling me back and staring at me from head to toe.

"You look wonderful," she laughed, her eyes lingering on my holly earrings. A knowing smile tugged her lips higher and she cupped my face. "It's so good to see you. Now, we'll talk more later. I'm going to bed now."

She kissed my forehead and bid everyone goodnight, and waved at Merric, before hugging Papa. Together they made their way back inside while I faced the man of the hour. He gave me a small smile, but the corners of his eyes crinkled, showing Santa's ever present happiness.

"Well done, young lady."

"Thank you, Santa, but you haven't even been inside yet."

He stepped forward and took my hands as he knelt before me. "I don't have to go inside to know you and everyone still here have done an excellent job. Merric gives Chip reports, and Chip forwards them to me. I'm impressed. Now, let's take a quick look inside before Mrs. Claus and I go to bed."

Mrs. Claus stepped forward and wrapped her arm around Santa's waist when he stood. "Santa is used to long nights, but I'm not. It's good to see you, Holly."

Merric led the Claus's inside, and I told Vixen and Lunar a quick hello before they took off with the sleigh. They'd be back tomorrow night to take Santa and Mrs. Claus home. They would have stayed, but at the moment we had nowhere to hide the sleigh.

Inside, Merric showed them the conference room and my office. Santa nodded his approval and we headed for the elevator. He had us stop at various floors on the way down, and after a quick look, he rejoined us. On the main floor, Jolly offered to walk them to the other building, but Merric stopped her by saying he was going that way and it would be safer. Santa agreed and led Mrs. Claus outside. Merric followed after giving me a goodnight hug, followed by a kiss.

"Well, so far so good," I murmured when the door closed behind them all. Noel had joined us since she'd been in my office when Santa had inspected it. She'd nearly fallen out of my chair when he'd stepped inside.

"Oh brother, Holly. If he didn't take up an issue with anything he saw tonight, I think you're safe." She shook her head and a large yawn escaped her. "By the way, Jolly invited me over for a slumber party tonight. And don't complain," she argued, sticking a finger in my face. "That bed of yours is big enough for the three of us."

"Jolly tried to take my face out this morning, and you want to add another person?"

"Suck it up buttercup. Now, let's head to bed. I'm bushed."

Noel led the way upstairs. Mama and Papa were already asleep when we entered the apartment so we tiptoed past their door. In my room, it didn't take long for all three of us to change and pile onto the bed. Jolly lost the race into bed and was stuck with the middle. Served her right for setting up a slumber party the night Santa arrived.

. . .

No arm woke me before my alarm. I'd been awake staring at the ceiling for hours listening to the light breathing of the girls sleeping beside me. Noel snored lightly and Jolly mumbled incoherently every few minutes before settling again. When I couldn't take another second of counting ceiling tiles, I climbed from bed and repeated yesterday morning's pattern, leaving the apartment before anyone else was awake.

This morning, I didn't get a chance to text Merric before I noticed the conference room's lights were switched on. Bright light filled the darker hallway and I peered inside. Santa sat at the head of the table scrolling through a tablet. A tired looking Merric sat beside him. His eyelids appeared heavy, and dark rings encircled his eyes. So, I wasn't the only one who couldn't sleep.

"Good morning, Holly," Santa greeted, tearing his eyes from the tablet. "Since we were awake, Merric and I decided to start the day early. I'm glad to have you join us. We just started, so please don't feel like we did this behind your back. We wanted you to sleep."

"It's okay. I couldn't sleep. What are we doing?" I sat on Santa's other side, across the table from Merric. He winked, and I blushed when Santa noticed, but he didn't comment.

"Merric was showing me the financials of the project and other paperwork. So far, everything looks to be in order. Now that you're both here, I want to discuss something else with you that has me concerned." He slid the tablet back to Merric, who eyed Santa with a wary expression. "I want to know exactly what happened the morning of your announcement about Merric's bloodline. Word for word."

It didn't take long to relate the experience to him. He wasn't kidding either. If we paraphrased, he asked us to tell him the exact wording as close as we could remember. When we finished, he leaned back in his chair and remained silent for several minutes.

"When Chip told me what happened, I was concerned that something that had been said or done was misinterpreted by the elves who left. Now I see that's not the case. This is disheartening, and I need to think on it. No elf should ever treat another elf, human, or any combination of the two like they did. I should have been more aware of this problem. I'm sorry you have had to endure this hardship, and your family as well, Merric. You can be rest assured I will get to the bottom of this."

"Thank you, Santa," Merric murmured.

For the next hour or so, Santa asked us questions, both about how we felt the job was progressing, and how the elves reacted to the job. Each question was met with an honest answer. When Mrs. Claus, Mama, Papa, and Jolly joined us, we began the tour.

Elves were already at work baking when we exited the elevator on the top baking floor. We'd already prepped Santa with the information that the last ovens were to be sent soon. Every elf stopped what they were doing when Santa stepped off the elevator, and those not from Christmas Village released giddy squeals, hopped in circles, or demonstrated some other form of excitement. While Santa was concerned about the work they did, he spent most of his time talking to each elf he met. He made sure each one knew he cared about them. That was nothing new to me or any of the other elves from the North Pole. We knew that was Santa's personality. It became apparent that the other elves weren't as aware of that.

The day flew by, and soon it was time for Santa and Mrs. Claus to depart. As a going away gift, I handed them a box of cookies and muffins for the trip home. When the sleigh took flight and was out of sight, I released a long, steady breath and let my muscles relax. My shoulders slouched, but I didn't care, especially when Merric's strong fingers worked to massage my tired shoulder muscles.

"Your family and Noel are in your apartment ready to celebrate our success, but I want a few minutes alone with you first. And I have something for you, but you have to come inside to get it."

"What is it?"

He took my hand and led me toward the stairs into the building. "It's a surprise, and you won't get it if I tell you what it is."

"You wouldn't tell me anyway."

"True."

Once inside, Merric led us to the stairs and we descended them to his office's floor. It wasn't surprising at that point that he led me straight to his office, but once inside, he closed the door. I arched an eyebrow at him, but he shrugged.

"I was hoping for some privacy. You know how elves are. I wanted to talk a little as well, but first, your surprise." He tugged me to join him beside his desk where he reached inside a drawer and lifted another cookie box sitting on a plate. I couldn't stop the bemused expression that crossed my face, causing him to chuckle. "I love your name. I love holly."

"I see that."

"Open it." He held the plate out to me so that I could open the lid of the cookie box.

Another jewelry box sat inside, and without question, I removed it from the cookie box, which Merric set down on the desk. This time when I opened it, my jaw popped open. Inside laid a gorgeous ring. A large ruby sat in the center and a ring of tiny emeralds encircled it. It was the most beautiful ring I'd ever seen in my life.

Looking to Merric, I found him kneeling before me and every inch of my body went on alert and my stomach twirled in giddy anticipation. He reached forward, took the box from my hand, and slipped the ring onto my left hand.

"I know that traditionally it's supposed to be a diamond, but the night I saw you wear rubies, I couldn't pass up giving you this ring. You sparkled brighter than any diamond I could give you. Holly, you make me happier than anyone ever has. Before I met you, I lived my life, but the moment I met you, you gave my life meaning. You showed me what love is, and I will never forget that. I can only hope that one day I'll be for you what you've become to me. You are my best friend, and I know it's fast, but Holly, will you marry me?" He took my hand and pressed a tender kiss to the back of it while I fought to find my voice.

"Merric, stand up you silly man," I laughed when I could speak. Tears slipped from my eyes, trailing wet streaks down my cheeks. He stood and wiped them away. "I love you so much. I don't care how fast this is. I know I'm meant for you, just as you're meant for me."

"So that's a yes?"

My head fell forward to rest on his chest as I laughed. "Yes, that's a yes. Yes, I'll marry you."

"Good. Now the real work begins."

"Like what?" I asked, stepping back to grin at him.

"Planning a wedding. After this project, that'll be a piece of cake." He winked to punctuate his bad joke, and I could only shake my head at him.

"I'm waiting, you know."

"Waiting for what?"

"For you to kiss me, elf man."

His boyish grin grew into a wide smile and his eyes fell to my lips. "Then let me oblige you."

Stepping forward, he set his hands on my hips and pulled me to him before wrapping one arm around my waist and intertwining his other hand into my hair. His lips crushed against mine in the most passionate kiss we'd shared yet. The best part was that he tasted like freshly frosted sugar cookies.

AUTHOR CHRISTMAS MESSAGE

As most, if not all, of my friends and family know, I'm a huge Christmas fanatic. It doesn't matter what time of year, you can find me listening to Christmas music, decorating Christmas ornaments, or asking if it's too early to set up my Christmas tree. For me, Christmas is the happiest time of year, and I truly believe it is a time when love is the strongest. I thank God for the opportunity I have to try and share that love with you through my words. In each of my Christmas novels, I hope to capture the importance of family, love, unity, and the peace that the season brings. May we all keep the love of Christmas in our hearts during this blissful season, but also throughout the year.

Merry Christmas,
Heather

ABOUT THE AUTHOR

Heather has a love for all things books, crochet, and Christmas. Oh, and hot chocolate, which makes an appearance in almost every book she's written. Can you spot the amazing cup of deliciousness in your next read? She also has a newly discovered love of trying new recipes. Most are great…some not as much.

When she's not writing, Heather can be found wandering the local cemetery to escape the apartment or sitting out on the back deck enjoying the fresh air. She loves everything paranormal or urban fantasy, especially if it has shifters in it. That's perhaps why most of her books have shifters in them.

Facebook Author Page: www.facebook.com/heatherkarnauthor
Facebook Group: www.facebook.com/groups/theweregalchronicles
Website: www.heatherkarn.com
Instagram: www.instagram.com/heatherkarnauthor
Amazon Author Page: https://www.amazon.com/Heather-Karn/e/B01JCXJLCI
Bookbub: https://www.bookbub.com/profile/heather-karn
Goodreads:
https://www.goodreads.com/photo/author/15555737.Heather_Karn
Newsletter: eepurl.com/cdbpkp

ALSO BY HEATHER

Standalones

Phoenix Awakened

Mate: Level 8

The Weregal Chronicles

Perfect Scents

Whitewash

Black Out

Redemption

Freedom

Unity

Gargoyle Collection

Gargoyle's Kiss

Gargoyle's Pixie

Gargoyle's Christmas

Christmas Collection

First Christmas

Cookie Christmas

Evergreen Christmas

Snowbound Christmas

First Blood Series

First Blood

Second Lineage

Third House

Zero Tolerance

Fourth Bunker

Negative Energy

First Blood Novel Series

A Very Necromancer Christmas

Stalking The Enemy Series

Freedom's Touch

Stalking the Magician

Demon Cleaved Series

Demon Fire

Dark Night Series

Dark of the Night

Black Cat Series

Black Cat's Curse

Druid's Healing Heart

Alpha King by Melanie Gilbert

By the age of nineteen, Ryske thought he'd be long gone from his pack in North Carolina. As an arctic wolf shifter in a pack of red wolves, he's an outcast. When he finds himself thrown into a portal to another world, he's in way over his head.

In a world where wolves once roamed with other shifters and mages, he competes to claim the princess's hand, making him instant enemies with Dirk, a lion shifter. But what choice does Ryske have other than to fight for the princess when a wolf, not a lion, is destined to be crowned Alpha King?

https://books2read.com/u/m2rVPk

Perfect Scents by Heather Karn

Joette McClane's life has gone from the happiest it could ever be to heartbreak with the deaths of her parents. Now living with her grandma and aunt, trying to put the pieces of her life back together, a school assignment shocks the life back into Joey - an essay on the weregals, a race of werecats who disappeared from the mountains of West Virginia nearly twenty years ago. As luck, or fate, would have it, not only does Joey stumble across the first weregal seen in years, but what Kev knows about Joey will turn her world upside down.

But Kev's not the only creature lurking in the West Virginia pines, and these other creatures might not be so friendly. Armed with her peculiar sense of smell, Joey and her friends set out to discover the truth behind these mysterious strangers who have their sights set on Joey.

Will the price of truth be too much to pay?

mybook.to/PerfectScents

Made in the USA
Monee, IL
29 August 2023

41753054R00115